EDUCATION, DEVELOPMENT AND NATION-BUILDING IN INDEPENDENT AFRICA

H. F. MAKULU

Education, Development and Nation-building in Independent Africa

A study of the new trends and recent philosophy of education

SCM PRESS LTD

334 00362 8

First published 1971
by SCM Press Ltd
56 Bloomsbury Street, London

© SCM Press Ltd 1971

Printed in Great Britain by
Northumberland Press Limited
Gateshead

Contents

Foreword

By His Excellency Dr K. D. Kaunda

Education in any society is a great boon – but it can also be a great curse if all it succeeds in doing in this society is to stratify it by creating an *élite* which is remote from the masses and which is conscious only of what society owes to it and not what it owes the society in which it has been brought up. This is the type of educational system that should be discouraged in any developing country where the crying need is for a body of properly trained men and women dedicated to the cause of putting service to society before self.

As in many other fields, independent Africa suffers from the very serious drawback of a dearth of printed material on its past, present and future activities and aspirations. Most of the publications that exist are those that have been compiled or written by foreigners who, although making purely subjective observations, usually proceed to make supposedly objective assessments of Africa's problems and diagnose solutions for them, which, in a number of cases, have ended up being far wide of the mark.

It is only now that, with the spread of education throughout most of the continent there has been an encouraging flow of learned works on various aspects of Africa's development by Africans themselves. This is a most welcome development, for one cannot get a better person to appraise, research in and pronounce authoritatively on how to best go about solving Africa's political, economic and social problems than the African himself. We are indeed now tiring of foreign 'advisers' and 'experts' who, day in and day out, keep announcing from the roof tops of their metropolitan centres what is best for Africa and how Africa *should* go about solving all the numerous ills (most of which are colonial relics) confronting her on both a collective and individual basis. The challenge to the sons and daughters of Africa is crystal clear – it has got to be met with determination and dedication if we are at all to assume successfully the role of improving the lot of our continent and, more specifically, make independent Africa a safer, happier and prosperous continent to live in. It is in the light of the foregoing remarks that I find this book a most welcome addition to the growing list of African writings on African problems by Africans themselves.

The subject itself that has been chosen could not have been more appropriate in the context of Africa's emergence from foreign domination, as she stands poised on the threshold of a 'technological take-off' with all the great promise that this holds for her people. In this phase, all countries will be pursuing certain distinct developmental goals in accordance with their national priorities. For these cherished goals to be attained, various factors have to interact effectively. Amongst these factors, trained manpower is bound to play a very significant role and is bound to dictate the pace at which this development is going to proceed. It is therefore most fitting that a meticulous analysis of its historical and philosophical background, present structure and planned future growth should be undertaken to ensure that the best possible policies are formulated and implemented in all those free countries of Africa which are in the forefront of the struggle against racism, as opposed to those countries where the majority are subjugated to the whims of those who claim racial superiority over them and who, when they offer them such basic services as education and health, do it in the most paternalistic and abhorrent manner!

The author is in a uniquely fortunate position in his questing role in examining the development of education as he himself has been actually involved in observing this very process both as a student in the very early missionary schools and latterly as a teacher. The author has also been extremely active in the Christian and ecumenical field. In addition to having been a member of the Board of Governors of the Mindolo Ecumenical Foundation (whose centre he was later to serve in the capacity of Vice Principal), the author has also served as Chairman of the All African Conference of Churches, as one of the Directors at the Ecumenical Centre in Bossey which comes under the World Council of Churches, as Chairman of the University Provisional Council and Teaching Service Commission, as a member of the Education Commission of Inquiry in 1960 and Judicial Service Commission from 1965 to date, till he was appointed, at the attainment of Zambia's independence, as a supernumerary and later a substantive Chairman of the Public Service Commission, which post he still holds.

It is quite obvious from the author's distinguished career that he is ideally suited to engage in a detailed appraisal of the interplay of the various motives that were behind the introduction of education in Africa by various groups and organizations. There were, for instance, the missionaries, who saw in educating the indigenous population a means of facilitating their conversion to Christianity; and there was the colonial administrator who saw in educating the local populace the means of producing a literate minion who would run errands for him as a domestic hand, messenger or orderly and, at best, a clerk! Both these approaches to education were based on the principle of giving to the African what was considered to be best for him and not necessarily an educational system which was in accordance with his cultural heritage and sociological environment and one that was aimed at projecting and promoting the African personality.

This is the challenge that is facing all developing countries in the world, in particular those in Africa. The age of the old unimaginative approach to education is over and the time has come for all young African countries to engage in serious appraisals of their existing educational systems with a view to overhauling them entirely and gearing them to the needs of the countries concerned. As I said earlier, trained manpower is crucial in a developmental process and it therefore follows that for overall economic planning to be assured of success it will have to be undertaken side by side with co-ordinated educational planning with clearly determined priorities.

There is no longer any place in Africa for the theoretical academician bent on researching into various aspects of man's environment which do not have much direct relevance to the development and/or improvement of man. This manner of highly theoretical research might be all right for the older countries which have had the benefit of centuries and centuries of education, but definitely not for emergent Africa. In fact, in some of these countries doctoral theses or dissertations have been written on so many subjects that younger aspirants to these high academic achievements are forced to have to choose topics which to the ordinary man in the street would not appear to be of any immediate human significance, for example, a thesis on the 'balancing of a fly on water surface'. In Africa, however, golden opportunities do exist, in that there are still vast fields of un-tapped knowledge which are crying out for more detailed research – research which will serve as the basis of the formulation of enlight-ened political, economic and social policies for the countries con-cerned.

This then brings me to the pressing need for the national univer-sities in each African country to avoid being ivory towers where dons theorize about the sorry state of whatever country they happen to be in and the world in general, whilst doing nothing positive to try and rectify whatever wrongs and ills they have identified. This means that the universities must so orientate their curricula as not to be out of touch with the national aspirations of the countries in which they operate. On the other hand, however, governments should on their part avoid seeing in the university academics and their students potential enemies waiting in the wings to pounce on to the stage and assume the reins of power! They must reassure the universities that they are an essential and integral part of the national develop-ment process and not a dissident minority committed to the course of destructive criticism.

The governments should therefore put the large pool of expertise available at such institutions to maximum utilization by involving them in various studies, research programmes, consultancy projects tied in with the governments' overall development plans. The aca-demics should on their part desist from being carried away by criti-cism for the sake of criticism in pursuance of mere intellectual satisfaction. They should instead live up to the trust placed in them by bringing themselves closer to the people, without whose sweat and toil they, the fortunate few, would never at all have attained the lofty positions from which they always tend to lecture the man in the street on every imaginable subject.

I cannot do better than repeat the message to all the African universities and seats of higher learning which I first gave to the first graduates of the University of Zambia at their Graduation Ceremony, when I reminded them as follows:

'The deprivations of your society are many, the poverty, ignorance and disease of your own society peep at you through the keyholes of your residence, your libraries and your lecture rooms. As you walk through the vaulty corridors of academic autonomy, know that there are men, women and children who will never be lifted from their lowly positions without your help.'

This is the collective challenge facing today's young Africans, and posterity stands to condemn them totally if they fail to live up to their responsibilities by assuming an insular approach to the role of education, and failing to take up as their mission the educational upgrading of all those capable of this in the societies in which they live.

The African governments on their part have, in accordance with the 'Final Report of the Conference of African States on the Development of Education in Africa' held in Addis Ababa in 1961, been making determined advances towards attaining universal primary education. Although the problems and obstacles being faced are very immense indeed and continue to proliferate day by day, the governments of independent Africa have performed admirably in this sphere of their development and it is my most sincere wish and hope that when 1980 comes, the story will be one of success all around and the stage will be set for the next battle in our continuing war against illiteracy by setting ourselves another target for achieving universality in secondary and technical education. We have the will-power and determination in abundant proportions, and with the necessary financial and other capital resources being available, success should not be too elusive a goal.

I would also like to identify myself with what the author has to say about the need to re-orientate the curricula, so that the subjects taught in the schools and in other seats of higher learning are those that are most relevant to the countries' developmental problems and national aspirations. It is only in this way that we shall ensure that the end products of our various educational systems in Africa will not be mere inferior Oxbridge replicas who pale into insignificance when confronted with practical problems, but men and women who are committed to what everyone in the nation is fighting for, men and women who know in which direction the nation is going, men and women who do not shun working on the land and in fact see in the land the ultimate solution to all the trials and tribulations plaguing most developing countries.

It is therefore absolutely essential to ensure that those charged with formulating the future educational blueprints for emergent Africa should realize that in our present developmental process in Africa two revolutions are taking place side by side – the technological and the agrarian. This therefore means that the educational planners will have to bias their curricula in favour of agricultural and technological subjects to ensure the emergence of a balanced trained manpower fully equipped to face and solve whatever problems confront their young countries.

We in Zambia have in a very humble way made a start in this direction, and it is my hope that financial and other resources permitting, we will steadily improve upon the existing number of agricultural and technical colleges and institutions, as time goes by, till such time that we can be in the happy position of declaring that self-sufficiency has been attained in the supply of trained manpower in these fields.

Further to the above, and in accordance with our philosophy of humanism, we in Zambia have ensured that the young should have inculcated in them the basic tenets and fundamental principles of this philosophy which centres on the importance of MAN in any human activity that takes place in this world. He is the means and end in any form of activity – be it political, economic or social. We have therefore decided that in order not only to produce an intelligent and learned citizenry but also a responsible and mature person, the philosophy of humanism should be incorporated into the curricula of the courses being organized at various educational institutions in the country. When projected further, this means that in every other country which has committed itself to a particular philosophy or strategy of economic, social or political development, the authorities should always ensure that this particular strategy is incorporated in the curricula of the country's educational institutions.

I am conscious of the fact that our detractors will jump at this and declare that this form of assisting the literate members of society is outright and open political indoctrination which should be discouraged. This could not be further from the truth, and such outbursts by our enemies should be treated with the contempt they deserve. After all, gone is the era when our so-called 'masters' used to dictate to us what was good for our development! These days, the only criterion of a good policy is whether the people for whom it was formulated and who will be called upon to put it into practice, accept it as a good one.

The educational task facing Africa today is immense and the problems seemingly insurmountable, but with the enlightened, progressive and dynamic political leadership that is to be found in the majority of African countries, I am confident that this challenge is going to be met with unsurpassable zeal and unfaltering determination, to the full benefit of all the next generations.

State House   Kenneth D. Kaunda
Lusaka   President of the Republic of Zambia
17th March 1971

Introduction

This inquiry sets out to discover, by an analysis of international conferences, seminars, consultations and other recent studies of education in Africa, what part education plays in the process of nation-building. Its scope is limited to Africa south of the Sahara, thus excluding North Africa and the Republic of South Africa, both of which have their own and different educational problems. Madagascar, on the other hand, is included, as it falls under French-speaking Africa.

This delimitation means that most of the countries which took part in the Conference of African States on the Development of Education in Africa, held at Addis Ababa in May 1961, are included. That conference is of particular importance because it was the first continent-wide conference of ministers of education from independent countries, and it took some far-reaching decisions and established some significant priorities. At the same time, it marks the beginning of a third and crucial period in the history of education in Africa.

The other two great periods in the development of education in Africa are analysed at the beginning of this book. The first of them is the time when education was part of the missionary effort of the Western church, which regarded education as an important evangelistic agent, and of the concern of colonial administration and Western philanthropy, which considered it to be necessary for the spread of Western civilization. This period lasted from about 1850 to 1900. The second, successive period, from 1900 to about 1950, is characterized by the insatiable hunger of the African peoples for education. The later part of this period is marked by the general take-over of education by governments from churches and missions.

Since the Addis Ababa conference, there has been a call for radical change in the direction of education. For the new nations of Africa, education must be directly related to economic development. 'Education is not only a good thing, it is a paying thing,' declares the Addis Ababa Report. At the conference it was claimed that money sensibly spent on education can be relied on to bring in a handsome profit. To this end, schools are considered to be at least as good an investment as industrial equipment, if not a better one. Furthermore, like industrial equipment, they need not necessarily be paid for out of the regular budget of the nation, but can be financed by government loans and other funding agencies. It is generally accepted that new nations in Africa cannot afford the luxury of unproductive, philosophically oriented education. The kind of education they want to plan for is that which can produce men and women who will help in the exploitation of the technical coming of age of Africa and in the task of nation-building.

However, the call for radical change in the direction and orientation of education issued by the African states in this way is bound to bring a number of problems. There is confusion in educational circles as to what kind of educational structures may come out of the new policies as envisaged by the conference. As the goals of education are considered, there is some apprehension about the too direct connection of education with economic development, the fear being that this might tend to turn education into a political instrument and reduce its freedom. Nevertheless, it must be recognized that one of the major tasks before the new nations in Africa is that of leadership and manpower development, and that education is rightly seen as the means by which this can be achieved. Among the fundamental questions to be discussed here are: What kind of educational structures are to be established which are in harmony with sound educational principles? What are the ways and means by which states in Africa can undertake the vast new plans while at the same time safeguarding their social, political and economic integrity? These are vital issues which will need immediate attention and direction in the next decade.

1

A Historical Survey of the Development of Education in Africa

The early history of education in Africa is the history of the planting of the Christian church. Education formed an integral part of missionary methods. For this reason it is important to search the records in the annals of the earliest missionary movement on the continent of Africa. From them we can see the significance and place of education in the manifold processes which have shaped the continent: the building of the Christian communities, the expansion of Western imperial influence through territorial acquisition and the establishment of strong and viable states, and finally the building of the new nations of Africa. There can be no doubt about the central role education has played in the development of the continent of Africa.

We must begin, however, by looking at education in its widest context. We believe that there were forms of education in Africa before Western nations came – the education for life which was part of the community life of the tribe in which the young generation was prepared for its role in society through organized patterns and systematic instruction. Tribal and traditional education was part of the social order of all communities. In the ancient empires such as those of Ghana, Mali, Songehi and Benin in the West of Monomotapa in East Central Africa, practical education of a considerably developed pattern was an essential part of social organization. The idea, therefore, of education for nation-building is by no means new; it is the form this education has taken which has differed in each phase of the history of Africa.

The nature of early tribal education differed greatly depending on the needs of a particular society and the demands of its environment. In societies in which people relied on hunting, the training was related to those skills which sharpened the senses of the youth and trained his responses to the stimuli of the environment. In the same way, among a fishing community a child was given the necessary orientation to make him a resourceful and effective member of that particular group. This education would continue from childhood to adulthood, punctuated by intensified tests during points of crisis in the cycle of the individual in accordance with his physical and psychological development. The main tests took place at the time of weaning (the end of this period is marked by a measure of severe training, including physical education) and at puberty, which is approximately between the ages of thirteen and fifteen. They took the form of *rites-de-passage*. Special instruction was also given at, and before, marriage. Rituals connected with all these phases of the cycle of life have educational value, because each has its own forms and formulae which have to be learned consciously in drama, folklore and in deliberate instructions by trusted and experienced adults of the community. In the same way, artistic procedures and formulae are handed on from one generation to another. The accumulated experience and the cultural artifacts are in this way preserved. The community in general and the special community of the initiation camp in particular are the schools of society. In these schools, the youth learns to accept the authority of the elders, and learns specific skills in hunting, fishing or cultivation. He also learns the wisdom of his tribe in stories and proverbs, forms of addresses and praises given in honour of the chief and other distinguished personal figures of the tribe. He learns what is the right behaviour in his community and what his responsibilities are as the successor of the older generation. In short, he has been prepared to play his part in the building of the nation. Nation-building today is, of course, a very much more complex process that requires intensive and diversified methods of preparation for its manifold tasks. Education, however, must still be the basic tool for this.

There is, however, no dynamic connection between these earliest forms of education and the present rise of nations. There are two reasons for this. First, development was interrupted by slavery and the slave trade which carried away millions of able-bodied men and women. Secondly, the expansion of colonial empires swept away the remaining strength of these civilizations and planted in their place a new technological civilization. This brought into Africa Western education and the dynamic power of the Christian gospel and its teaching, which have together gradually transformed the entire continent.

Education in the early church in Africa, 1450-1750[1]

The first entry of Western education into Africa was not, in fact, deliberate; it was introduced in the form of evangelism and as part of Western missionary enterprise. Building church schools for the purpose of creating literate Christian communities was begun at a very early stage in the Congo, in what is today Angola, by the Dominican and Jesuit orders who followed on the tracks of the early Portuguese navigators and explorers who operated with the support and under the patronage of the Christian King of Portugal, John II, whose vision and indomitable spirit led to the penetration of Africa. One of the motives for this expansion was to spread Christianity, and it was therefore only natural that from the beginning Portuguese settlements should also be centres for the Christianization of the inhabitants with whom the explorers came into contact.

The early forms of preaching and administration give ample evidence of the beginning of an educational process. The expedition of Diago Cao, beginning in 1484, is of particular interest in this respect because it was on one of his voyages that Diago Cao introduced the native African to Western civilization. He is a good example of an early explorer whose aims included the spread of the Christian faith, and through this education. His method, however, was primarily that of educating Africans away from Africa, rather than on their own continent.

Visiting the Lower Congo, Diago Cao was impressed by the potentialities for the spread of the Christian faith, for the introduction of Western civilization and for the expansion of the Portuguese empire and trade areas generally. Consequent upon successful negotiation and good relations with the African King of Congo, Diago Cao took with him on his return to Portugal a number of African men as a proof to the King of Portugal of his exploration.

They were received with great hospitality by King John II, who commanded that they be instructed in the Christian faith and should learn the Portuguese language. It is said that after a few months of instruction the men became proficient in Portuguese, were baptized and given Christian names. The next year, Diago Cao returned to Africa with the Congolese. The party proceeded into the interior, to King Mbanza-Kongo's capital, where they were well received. The men were laden with gifts from the Portuguese King to the King of Congo, but perhaps the greatest gift that they brought back with them was their new experience.

The King accepted baptism and sent away all his wives but one. His name was changed to John and that of his remaining wife to Eleanora; one of his sons, the heir apparent, was named Alphonso, and the King's capital was renamed San Salvador. Mbanza sent a request to King John II for missionaries to come and teach his people. It is said that Alphonso was quick at learning new things, even though he was not young, and soon mastered the Portuguese language and understood the theory and practice of law. Later Alphonso sent a group of Congolese youth, including his son, to Portugal to be educated. Henry, as Alphonso's son was named, studied in Lisbon and was ordained a priest. In 1518 he was made assistant bishop of Utica. This was the highest position any African had reached.

Lack of information on the continuation of this system of education outside Africa makes it clear that the failures were too many and discouragement rather than encouragement seems to have been the order of the day. We do not hear more of the successes of native Africans until the Jesuits and White Fathers establish seminaries in Africa. The earlier failures do not, however, seem to have provided a lesson for Protestant missions who, as we shall observe, made strenuous efforts to create African leadership by sending selected African youths to be educated in Europe. While some of these youths excelled in their work in European schools, there were also a number of pathetic cases of insecurity and tragic disappointment. The question that still looms large among educationists in Africa and in Western countries is that of the best place for educating the youth of Africa. The answer seems to us to be that education in the early and formative years of the African youth should be given in Africa, allowing for specialist training and research to be done, where necessary, in countries outside Africa where more facilities are available. This is evidently the direction in which thinking on education is going among many African educationists, and this fact is reflected in the plans and provisions for education now being made.

The determination of African states to create opportunities for full education within Africa up to university level cannot be doubted. There is evidence of this everywhere in Africa, despite the fact that it may be more expensive to provide such educational facilities in Africa than to send students overseas for the same type of education.

Catholic missions in the nineteenth century

In the Lower and Upper Congo during the nineteenth century, the next really significant period of missionary expansion, the most active Catholic order in establishing monasteries, churches and schools was that of the Fathers of the Holy Ghost. The following calendar shows the progress which this order made and some of its modest achievements:

1842   Vicariate of Gabon, West Coast. Evidence of monastery, which included among the staff one native priest, seven native brothers and forty-one catechists.

1865   Portuguese Congo. The old Capuchin mission was revived and reconstituted by the French Fathers of the Holy Ghost. There were twelve native seminarians, ten native brothers and twenty-four catechists.

1886   Loango River. Monastery and seminary which included one native priest, eight native seminarians, seventeen native brothers and sixty catechists.

1890   Ubanghi (Upper French Congo) monastery: there were some African brothers and fourteen catechists.

In 1907, the White Fathers also had a school for catechists with seventy-three pupils, a lower grade seminary with fourteen pupils and a higher grade seminary with one student. Catechists, the most numerous group, were those leaders who after some instruction in reading, writing and counting became teachers and were used for teaching in schools and conducting preparation and bible classes. They are said by an almost contemporary source to 'render very valuable service to the missionaries; they are always selected from among the cleverest and best trained of young native Christians'.

In Nigeria, Catholic missions did not fare too well. The main reason for this lack of success was that Northern and Western Nigeria were under the influence of Moslems. Another underlying factor was that, unlike the Catholic-oriented states of Lower and Upper Congo, Nigeria did not give Catholic missions a monopoly for evangelization or a special privileged position, and Protestant churches had long established themselves there. In the period from 1900, Catholic mission schools were established at Calabar, the administrative seat of Eastern Nigeria, and at a number of mission outposts. In all these places, churches and schools were reported to have attracted large crowds. In South and Central Africa, too, schools were said to be filled to overflowing. Mission schools and mission stations were established near the large towns of Bulawayo and Salisbury in Rhodesia. Numerous outposts and 'bush schools' were also established. Training of catechists was well organized, supported by a lower grade seminary at Chishawasha near Salisbury and at one other centre. In all these, the most active Catholic missionary order was the Jesuits, who were great pioneers in education. It must be said, however, that no attempt was made to train the indigenous African at a level similar to that in the Lower Congo, and for a long time there was no significant progress in this respect. The Protestant missions, however, did not seem to do any better.

The role of Protestant missions in education

The missionary motivation for promoting education varied only in detail among the different denominations. The underlying reason for this was the pessimistic attitude some of the early missionaries adopted when confronted with difficult African communities. Some gave up hope of converting adult natives and saw education of the children as the only solution. The emphasis in educational development did, however, differ somewhat between the Roman Catholic and the Protestant missions. Whereas for the Catholic missions the aim was to provide moral and religious education and to bring Christian influence to bear upon pagan communities, in the Protestant missions there was a strong emphasis on the training of the young by giving them a limited liberal education, the hope being that they would in this way create well-prepared, well-instructed and proven congregations.

For Protestant missions, education and the building of schools, hospitals and centres for elementary industrial training were all integral parts of evangelism. In their case, missionary work was to go hand in hand with the establishment of educational, medical and industrial centres. The earliest such establishments are to be found in what is now the Republic of South Africa. As this is outside the area of Africa covered in the present study, we shall not concern ourselves with the work of missions there. In general, the missionary pattern of operation consisted more or less of numerous preaching posts; hundreds of elementary and primary schools, one or more secondary schools, sometimes a bible school or theological college; several dispensaries, possibly a central hospital including elementary medical education, and one or more industrial training centres. These, taken together, added up to a huge system of all-round education.

The history of modern Protestant mission begins in 1792 with William Carey of the Baptist Association. Although his missionary work was wholly devoted to India, his inspiring and challenging accounts of the work of evangelism in new areas set many men's hearts aflame. The launching of the missionary movement is an important event not only in the history of the church in Africa but also in the history of technological development and educational expansion, which together have been the sequel to the process of the social and political revolution in Africa. The missionaries were determined to make Africa Christian, and education was an inseparable part of their evangelistic method. The 'challenge' of the Dark Continent brought into being numerous Christian organizations which formed themselves into missionary societies, among which the most active were the Baptist Missionary Society (established in 1792), the Edinburgh and Glasgow Missionary Society (established in 1796), the London Missionary Society (established in 1795) and the Church Missionary Society (established in 1799). The history of the Church Missionary Society, especially in West Africa, is a history of educational advance, and this society was connected with some of the early ventures in educating Africans. The establishment of the Bible Society in

1804 also had important significance for education as it promoted the circulation of the scriptures. The translation of portions of the scriptures involved a great number of indigenous Africans and was in itself an educational process of great significance. The demand for the bible in Africa has been phenomenal, and the bible has been a book of tremendous influence in the lives of Christians and non-Christians alike.

Other missionary societies which played important parts in educational development followed on in the early nineteenth century. Among them were the Wesleyan Missionary Society in 1813, the American Bible Society in 1816, the Church of Scotland Missionary Committee and numerous other foreign mission boards of the most important denominations of England, America, Germany, Sweden, Norway and France. All these missionary societies sent out men and women whose aim was to meet the need of the whole man; priests and pastors, doctors and nurses, educationists and teachers, technicians and agriculturalists – in short representatives of most aspects of the Western civilization of that time.

The general practice of most of these missionary groups was to create new communities of those who had been converted. The main reason for this was to move them out of a heathen environment into a homogeneous community of Christians. Mission stations and compounds were created, the majority of them on feudal patterns. Usually the whole community centred upon the 'mission' house which was often built upon a prominent site or hill, in order to assist the missionary to replace to some extent the role of the tribal chief. The second most important building would be the church, and the third the school. In most cases these schools would be boarding schools, supervised by the missionary educationist or the missionary's wife. The mission compound and the mission community stood in contrast with the communities around them. Close association with Christianity more often than not offered an attractive way of living and privileges in the form of education, medical services and industrial training. Some of the tribesmen who were converted came for the fascination of the white man's knowledge and the promise of a better life rather than because of a faith and understanding of Christian teaching. Education, more than anything else, was the compelling factor, since education was seen as the white man's key to success. Thus while the missionary motivation for education was evangelism, for the African it was a way of entering into the mysteries of Western technological civilization. Christianity and the missionary movement of Western churches have together contributed to the liberalization of the mind and spirit of the African and are therefore partly responsible for the social and political revolution of modern Africa.

A brief sketch of Protestant missionary involvement in the process of educational development in some typical areas may be added here. Because of the numerous branches of the Protestant denominations involved in mission work and education it is not easy to give a chronological sequence to this development. However, it is the case that each of the various missionary societies was carrying on the task of missionary expansion and building schools and hospitals independently. In many areas 'comity' agreements were reached by which each mission confined its work to one area, usually serving one homogeneous group, as an attempt to find a solution to unnecessary competition. The comity in some instances sealed the fate of particular tribes, since some of the missionary societies were determined to give of their best in education and other services, while others were too conservative and not sufficiently well endowed with resources of material and personnel to meet educational and medical needs adequately. The end result was that certain tribes had educational advantages over others and today have come out better equipped for leadership in many fields in the new societies than others.

On the West coast, the oldest institution is Fourah Bay College, Freetown, which gained new status as The University College of Sierra Leone in 1960. It was established in 1827 on the initiative of the Church Missionary Society. This school served the Gold Coast and Nigeria, which were then known as British West Africa, and which had been under the Sierra Leone administration up to 1874. Many men from the Gold Coast and Nigeria were sent to Fourah Bay College for higher education.

In Nigeria, a remarkable experiment was made with an African, Samuel Adjai Crowther, who, after some training at Fourah Bay College, was sent to England for further theological education. In 1864 he was consecrated a bishop, the first indigenous African bishop of the non-Roman Catholic church, but lack of genuine personal fellowship with others of his interests and calibre made his work difficult, and the experiment was not a success. The failure of this

educated African raises again the question of the wisdom of educating Africans away from Africa.

The examples we have given of the missionary motivation for
the introduction of Western education in Africa lead us to the conclusion that the by-product of this process, namely education for
enlightenment and civilization, had overshadowed the main objective
of evangelism. Missionary education had thus brought in the dynamic
force of knowledge and had made enormous strides in liberating the
African mind and body. By creating the desire for education, the
missions had made enormous strides in liberating the African mind
and body. By creating the desire for education, the missions had indirectly fostered the needs of the African revolution. The greatest
of their contributions is that they provided Africa with leaders who
have come to assume responsibility in the building of new nations.
In short, the real foundation of education in Africa is the fervent
missionary movement of the nineteenth century. This foundation
having been laid, it was easy for the new system of education now
built by the colonial governments to operate. The church did not,
however, retire from the scene. Many missions still continue to participate in the development of education in full co-operation with
the governments concerned.

The period of transition

This period of missionary instruction in education leads into the next,
when the basis of education becomes the strengthening of colonial
administration and the widening of the African's horizon. In the
next chapter we shall look more closely at the development of education in Africa, a development that brought colonial governments to
the realization that education was too powerful an instrument to be
left in the hands of other agencies without some guidance and control. Generally, this development takes place in the period after 1900
and especially after the First World War. Interest on the part of
colonial governments in the planning of education brought two
important elements into the development. First, it unified the various
educational efforts of the missions, brought in some regular system
and laid down standards of instruction by means of supervision and
grants-in-aid. Secondly, there emerged a system of education in which

there was close co-operation between the government and missions. The vision of the great missionary explorer, David Livingstone, was becoming more and more evident – Africa was being opened up to commerce, education and Christianity to complete the impact of Western civilization. The policy of education had become more or less defined. It was education for development, development of the African child to the maximum of his ability in order to enable him to be useful to the community and to himself. Colonial administration had become a diversified service and demanded the training of junior officials to assist the colonial administrators in the task of introducing Western government machinery into the new colonies. In the British, French and Belgian systems, indigenous Africans were thus trained to be clerks, hospital orderlies, nurses and teachers. The catechist as the bearer of education was replaced by the trained teacher, who had often been trained through the pupil-teacher system, which trained by practice rather than by theory. More and more schools were established both in the new urban centres and in the villages.

The period was well characterized by Albert Victor Murray, an eminent educationist with experience in both the theory and the practice of education. His book on education in Africa, *The School in the Bush* (Longman, London 1929), is a critical study of the theory and practice of education in Africa. Murray expresses concern over the forces that are beginning to play upon the life of the African. His major contribution to the field is his evaluation of the strategic place of the African teacher despite his sometimes inadequate training. For Murray, the important thing was not what the organization of education tried to do, but rather the role of the African teacher himself. He was the key man in the whole educational system. *The School in the Bush* was a challenge to educational authorities, government and missions alike, as it brought out the stark truth about the systems, administration and whole ethos of education. But Murray was expressing a dissatisfaction which was already felt among educationists.

The strategic place of the village teacher was now being recognized as of particular importance in the system of education. The training of village teachers was becoming a priority. In 1930, a group of secretaries of British missionary societies gave a report of their study of the problem.[2] This group considered the village school to be the most important unity in African education because it is both the educational institution and a centre for creative community life. To this end, therefore, the teacher must be a leader in the community. The school, the group argued, 'must belong to the community'; it must help in the development of rural economy, particularly in agriculture; it must make village life interesting and must inculcate in the child habits of industry and respect for the traditions and customs of his people.

The group emphasized that the training of teachers should therefore have a double objective, 'to produce men qualified to be moral and spiritual leaders of the village community' and 'to produce well-trained teachers' equipped with the necessary teaching techniques. The teacher 'must study the history of his own people, their customs and organization of society' as well as philosophy of education and methods of teaching.

This picture serves to show the extent to which the missionary societies became more and more involved in the problems of educational organization, consequent on their effort to meet the great demand for popular education. This demand was both quantitative and qualitative, and required new schools to be built and new teachers to be trained and supervised. As years went by, these demands increased the load on the missions to such an extent that education almost swamped the evangelistic aspect of missionary work.

NOTES

1. The Catholic Encyclopedia has been the main source of information used in the preparation of this part of the survey. General histories of Africa lack information about this period, and where they do try to deal with it, they are scanty and rather patchy. For the following details, see especially vol. IV, 1913.

2. 'The Training of Village Teachers in Africa', *International Review of Missions*, April 1930, p. 231.

2

Education for Development and Advancement

As educational needs increased and the demands on the missions multiplied, the burden became too heavy for them. As we have seen in the previous chapter, governments were generally and increasingly getting involved in the education of the African. The first step was that of encouraging missions to continue to provide education. This encouragement differed in method from region to region. In some territories, for example in the Belgian Congo, the government officially placed education, including the greater part of its planning, in the hands of the church. In the Belgian Congo, the Roman Catholic Church was entrusted with the task of educating the African, a responsibility which was later extended to some of the Protestant missions. In other territories, the government gave part grants-in-aid and assumed some right of supervision and regulation of the curriculum. Of particular importance in this period is the fact that education was gradually beginning to be understood as a much broader process than the teaching of the scriptures in preparation for membership of the church, and the notion of the three Rs was seen as too limited to lead to development and advancement. This led to the gradual introduction of other subjects, such as geography, history and physical education. However, as long as the different Christian denominations continued to have a monopoly in education, confusion and lack of precision in aims and policies continued. Furthermore, the development of education did not proceed at the same rate in all the territories of Africa, nor did it go through the same stages. The greatest progress was made in what was then British West Africa, where there was a phenomenal increase in the establishment of schools, including some with secondary education.

During the period up to about 1930 there was a general difference in the objectives of the education given by the missions and the colonial administrators. In some areas a third party came into the controversy – the European settlers. This divergence of ideas about what kind of education was to be given to the African caused stagnation in its development. The fear of competition for jobs and demands for equal rights pushed some white settlers to extremes, and they asserted that education of the native should not be of the kind that would make him forsake his place in the tribal community. If he must be educated, his education should not encourage him to be anything beyond a good servant. The missionary, by and large, still clung to the objective of training for church membership. On the other hand, administrators were anxious to introduce the kind of education that would make the African useful in the administration of the territory and in community development. There were many outstanding exceptions in all the three groups, but the trouble was that they were all concerned with what was good for the African and not with what the African himself wanted. In fairness, however, it should be said that the missionary educators were more often far-sighted, and among them have arisen some of the greatest educational philosophers, who have given a strong foundation to African education.

It has become increasingly clear that the new African states will want to make education a secular responsibility. They will also resist external influences to interfere with the policy and planning of education. This will bring to a definite end, at least in a good number of countries, the concept of partnership with the missions and the church in education. The Conference of Ministers of State on the Development of Education recognized the role churches and missions have played in the development of education, but there is no word of commitment on their part for partnership with the church in the future planning of education. This was borne out in a discussion by African educationists at the Conference on Higher Education at Tananarive in 1962, in which they expressed the desire to exclude religious instruction from the secondary school curriculum. This does not necessarily mean that the church and missions will close their schools or that there will be no room for church schools; it only means that the whole policy-making and direction of education will be directly controlled by the state. Many state authorities realize this and accept it. The church will be regarded as a supplementary rather than as a complementary agent in education. This position removes churches and missions from the formal control of education. The only way in which their influence can continue to be felt in the system of education is by the character and calibre of those who come out of the few church schools that they may be allowed to continue to operate.

On the level of educational planning, the past has seen close collaboration between the church and the government, and many colonial governments consulted with the missions in the planning of their educational policy. In many conferences on education, an important place was given to the representative of the opinions of the church. Sometimes it was the missions which called the government's attention to the problems of education. A good example of this was the representation of the International Missionary Council which led to the setting up of an Advisory Committee on Education in the Colonies in 1924. This advisory committee produced a memorandum in 1925 in which principles for educational policy in Tropical Africa were worked out. Among these principles was that of the responsibility of the government to control education, but always to co-operate with other educational agencies. Through this advisory body the Secretary of State for the Colonies was always in touch with, and well informed about, the developments in education in the dependent territories. However, with the independence movement changes have taken place in the responsibility and concern for educational planning. Education, like other aspects of development, is now planned in Africa by Africans themselves.

In the countries of French West Africa the situation is slightly different. One of the problems which influenced the French policy on education there was that of the existence of large numbers of Moslems who would not allow their children to enter Christian Mission schools, and who insisted on the right of their children to be taught the Koran. The result of this was that in territories with large Moslem communities a new kind of school appeared on the educational scene, namely the state school. This policy was established by the labours of General Faidherbe, who became administrator of Senegal in 1854. It was he who instituted 'lay' schools in order to meet the educational needs of Moslems. This move was a significant one, and created a change in the educational policy of French-speaking Africa. By 1900 there were over seventy state schools in French territories. After this period a common system of schools ranging from elementary schools through advanced primary schools to professional schools was introduced in this part of Africa. A system of school supervision was established. Advanced primary schools were established in most principal towns of the territories. In addition there were advanced professional schools such as the École de Medicine in Dakar in Senegal and the École Technique, which supplied the government with trained artisans. Institutions or classes of secondary school standard in which pupils reached the same standards as in metropolitan France were also established. As far as the government was concerned, this education was to be directed towards the introduction of French culture and in general to the spread of Western civilization. The declared aim was to raise a nucleus of *élite* who would be partners in the administration of the government. A dramatic change in the government-mission share of education there took place between 1900 and 1910. Whereas in 1900 there were only seventy state schools with an enrolment of some 2,500 pupils,[1] in 1910 there were a large number of state schools with an enrolment of 11,484 pupils; the missions and other private schools had 2,962 pupils. In 1938 the state schools had 56,135 pupils, the mission schools had 12,281. In addition, there were 63,734 pupils in Moslem schools.[2] Mission schools had become 'private schools', and consequently had come under the stipulation of 1922, which required, among other things, an authorization by the government for the opening of such schools, that the teaching must be in French, and that the teachers must have the same qualifications as government teachers. In these circumstances it was difficult for new mission schools to open and for some of those established to continue.

In the territories administered by Belgium, that is the Congo and Ruanda Burundi, the policy was different again. Full monopoly of education was given to the Roman Catholic Church. Even where schools were built by the government, they were staffed by Roman Catholic teachers. Missions were divided into two classes, 'national missions' and 'foreign missions'. Only national missions (Roman Catholic) received grants. In Portuguese territories, education was considered as a means of spreading the Portuguese language and culture. Europeans and assimilated Africans were provided for in state schools; the rest of the native people were either left illiterate and uneducated or the missions provided for their education. Roman Catholic missions received more encouragement than Protestant, but Protestant mission education was of a very high standard, and among the few well-educated are those who have gone through Protestant missions.

In this survey there are many gaps for reasons of brevity. We should, however, mention in passing two important countries in Africa which have not been under any one of the metropolitan or colonial powers, but which have given serious attention to the problems of education as an important aspect of nation-building. They are Ethiopia and Liberia. Ethiopia has had many difficulties in the planning of education because of its large population and backward economy, but it has had education related to the church, and the college in Addis Ababa is one of the oldest in Africa. Liberia has had a long educational tradition and, in spite of the enormous physical and economic obstacles, there has been remarkable progress in education in recent years. The University of Liberia is one of the oldest centres of higher learning in Africa.

Aims and objectives of education during the period of colonial administration

In the early stages, the object of education in Africa was the spreading of European civilization. In consequence, all those tribal institutions which seemed to be contrary to this were either discouraged or suppressed. The tendency was to measure every part of African life by European standards. This ignorance was challenged by the studies of social anthropologists who gained a better insight and understanding of African society, its institutions and customs. After the First World War the idea developed that African tribal life had distinctive values which no other system could replace without bringing instability and a sense of insecurity to the African peoples. Educationists now sought to develop this into an educational principle, namely that education should prepare the African child to use the best elements out of his tribal environment and to transform it by bringing into it what he had received from Western education. The emphasis was therefore placed on the use of the child's experiences. What this involved in the actual planning of education was that there was a definite shift from the idea of mere assimilation of Western ideas to that of development from within. It was generally agreed that the teaching of the three Rs did not constitute a lasting education aimed at the 'whole man' which would be useful in life.

This philosophy, however, did not become popular because of the African's insatiable hunger for education. Education for him symbolized power, for it was seen as the door to the European's technological mysteries. Education became identified with the escape route from manual work and from the old tribal discipline. The white-collar job mentality entered the mind of the educated African child. His masters, the white teachers and their countrymen, did not set a better example as they appeared only in supervisory roles. Thus authority and privilege were associated with education.

The period between 1918 and 1930 was crucial. The pressure on missions to provide education was becoming greater every year. Rumblings about the disinterested attitude of the government were going on both in Africa and in Europe and America. This was a period when the system of education had to advance or break down. Confusion as to the aims in African education was apparent. The question of the obligation of the government to take responsibility for education was being discussed. The importance of the situation is seen in the readiness of the missions to accept the suggestion of the American societies that the experiences Americans had in the planning and carrying out of education among the negroes would be valuable in Africa. This led to the coming of the Phelps-Stokes Commission, which visited Africa in 1922 and 1925. Similarly, the British Colonial Office concern about this crisis is shown by its willingness to accept advice on education in Africa. This led to the creation of the Advisory Committee on Native Education in British Tropical African Dependencies, in which missions had an important share. The function of this committee, as we have already indicated, was to advise the Secretary of State for the Colonies on the development of education in Africa.

In the task of making an appraisal of the different attempts that were made to clarify the object of education in Africa, it is useful to study the reports of some of the important commissions on education in Africa. Of particular importance to this study are two commissions, the Phelps-Stokes Commission mentioned above, and the Nuffield Foundation and the Colonial Office *Report of the Commission on African Education. A Study of Educational Policy and Practice in British Tropical Africa*, 1953. These commissions were specifically concerned with the study of policy, systems and aims of education in countries which were British dependencies. The following analysis of their reports attempts to show how the process of education has had to change its direction in order to move towards the expected political change.

The Phelps-Stokes Fund: Commission Report [3]

The report opens with optimism about the prospect and potentialities of educational development in Africa. It discusses the old myth of the 'Dark Continent', which the commission attributes to a misunderstanding of the continent itself and its people. This note is sounded at the very outset, where the report declares: 'Africa is not the Great Dark Continent, but the Continent of Great Misunderstandings.[4]

The more significant points in the Phelps-Stokes Report are related to the importance of adaptation. That education should be adapted to conditions of life is the prominent feature of the report. It decries the attempts to drive the African child into the pre-conceived forms of education of Western countries with the adoption of Western cultural institutions and usages. The main result of this policy is that education becomes mechanical, with little meaning to the inner personality. Learning seems to be for some utilitarian purpose, and individual development is only incidental. For missions and churches the most significant thing in the Phelps-Stokes Report is the strong plea it makes for religious and moral education as the basis of a lasting education. This was an important point, because in previous years a controversy had raged between governments and missions about the place of religious instruction in schools. Governments were generally willing to listen to the advice of such a high-powered team of world-renowned educationists.

Another contribution of the Phelps-Stokes Commission was the scheme worked out by Dr Jesse Jones to provide opportunity for observation of educational methods among the negroes of the USA, particularly of community development and health centres, but also of work in universities and colleges. Teachers were sent from all parts of Africa to the USA to enable them to observe and study the system of education and methods of giving maximum assistance to rural teachers and schools which usually operated under crowded conditions with poorly trained teachers.

In the years that followed, the American-developed Jeanes teacher system was brought to Africa. The importance of this system was that it helped in upgrading the standard of teaching by supervision and demonstration – a very important service where the bulk of the teachers are barely educated, let alone trained, a condition that was prevalent in Africa.

During the second phase in the development of education in Africa, that is, the period we have already described as the period of 'popular education', an attempt was made to introduce into the school curriculum subjects which give expression to the natural environment and the needs of the child's own community, stories and folk-lore, tribal and traditional dances, and instruction in local handicrafts. All these seemed to be new and progressive innovations in the 1920s and 1930s. In fact, however, some of them have become obsolete and meaningless in the conditions of rapid social and cultural change that have taken place. For example, the conventional lessons in African handicrafts teach a child the productive process in which a hand-made basket takes days or weeks to weave, but at the same time there are cheap wares of superior quality on the market. This kind of educational development does not seem to take account of the changed conditions in which the child lives. If the aim of education is the development of the individual to his maximum capacity for complete living in society, the pressures which come upon him must be watched. These pressures result sometimes from normal social and economic changes and sometimes from social and political upheavals which necessitate adjustment.

The views of the Phelps-Stokes Commission on the organization of education make one point clear, that educational organization or the system and methods of this organization are dependent on such factors as the type of education itself and the educational needs to be achieved, as well as on the economic, social and cultural conditions of the particular area in which the system operates. In view of the sweeping changes that have begun to take place and the significance of the influences of new nations on the educational systems, it may be added that political conditions also affect the organization of education. The report lists the objects of education as: the training of the masses of the people; the education of future leaders; the training of those who must pass the conventional tests required by professional schools.

On secondary education the report emphasized that this was the determining factor in any plan for educational development. Other levels of education fall or stand on the basis of the extent to which the secondary education system has developed. It is also to be emphasized that the rate of development in higher education has not been as fast as the African revolution has made necessary. During the time of the Phelps-Stokes Commission on Education in Africa, there were only two institutions of full university status in Africa south of the Sahara (excluding the white universities in the then Union of South Africa): Fourah Bay College in Sierra Leone in West Africa and Fort Hare in Cape Province in South Africa.[5] (At the end of 1962 there were about twenty institutions of post-secondary level, with a student body of about 10,000, but a greater number than this was enrolled in universities outside Africa. This is evidence of the crisis in education in Africa – a crisis that was attended with problems which could not be solved merely by increasing higher education facilities, but rather by the breaking of the educational vicious circle, possibly at the secondary level point. The key to the solution seems to lie in a careful and imaginative planning which takes serious account of the social, economic and political realities.)

The commission called attention to the need for clear objectives in education in order to build effective systems of education and pointed in the direction education should take if it were to be of lasting value. Education in Africa needed to take into account the child's environment and the role in society which he was to play. Often this curriculum was in contradiction to these aims. The commission drew attention to the importance of language. The use of the mother tongue was essential for the development of the child's latent capacity. Notwithstanding the need to adapt education to the environment and the needs of the African, there was no doubt about the importance of introducing him to the new technological development that was bound to make an overwhelming impact on the continent in the years that were to follow. The commission in its stress on the training of character put religious and moral instruction as priorities in the curriculum, as it considered these to be of primary importance in the child's development, especially in Africa. Academic subjects such as health instruction, agriculture, and physical education were considered of secondary importance, while crafts and home economics formed a third group. The commission urged close cooperation between government and mission in the task of developing education in the years that were to follow and urged that there be more co-operation among the missions, which were often working in competition.

In conclusion of this brief survey, it must be emphasized that the Phelps-Stokes Commission was an important landmark in the development of education in Africa. Modern education in Africa began as a response to the challenge of the Phelps-Stokes Commission and its findings. The report led to the re-thinking of educational policy. The British Colonial Office created an Advisory Committee on Education for the purpose of endeavouring to meet the crisis which the Phelps-Stokes Commission had revealed. This led to the subsequent preparation of two Memoranda on Education in British Tropical Africa, on the basis of which the present structures of education are founded. Among the many results of these memoranda, three important features stand out: first, the creation of central and local advisory committees in all countries in British Tropical Africa; secondly, the increased popularity of education as it became the direct responsibility of the government; thirdly, the close relation of education with African life through the use of African languages in school and the production of books specially designed for African schools.

It had become clear to the advisory committee in London that there was need for a constant watch on the developments in education. This conviction had been emphasized by the Phelps-Stokes Commission. The commission had also indicated the direction of future studies. Consequently, the interests of the Nuffield Foundation in the development of African education resulted in a co-operative effort with the Colonial Office which led to the sending of two teams to study educational needs in West, East and Central Africa, a task which was completed by the epoch-making conference at Cambridge in 1952. This conference was attended by educators from many countries in Africa, both European and African. It was, in fact, the first time that such a gathering had taken place.

The Cambridge Conference on African Education, 1952

The main objective of the Cambridge Conference was to review the educational system in Africa. The general and widespread criticism of the system of education at the time was that it was superficial and bookish. The report made two points which sum up these criticisms: first, that the education being given was inadequate and that it was unable to carry sufficient numbers up to a level where the result of schooling would begin to be of much value to the child; secondly, that the educational system had failed to replace effectively the African life which it, together with other Western forces, had destroyed. This was evident everywhere in Africa.[6] It was being admitted at the end of the Second World War that there was a real crisis in education in the territories administered by Britain in Africa, but there was no unanimity on the method of meeting this crisis. There were two schools of thought; one suggested that the answer lay in establishing more schools, the other suggested that the poor quality of the existing schools was at the root of the problem and that the solution lay in the raising of standards in these few schools, so as to provide a worthwhile education for the few who had the chance to go to them.

Before the conference, two study groups had visited Africa for the purpose of getting local opinion and for the appraisal of the educational situation. One group visited West Africa: Gambia, Sierra Leone, Gold Coast (Ghana) and Nigeria; the second group visited East and Central Africa: Nyasaland, Northern Rhodesia (Zambia), Tanganyika (Tanzania) including Zanzibar, Kenya, Uganda and British Somaliland. The reports of these two groups provided the basis for the Cambridge Conference.

The West African Study Group

The report of the West African group showed concern for the broad principles of education. While it surveyed the position and went deeply into the fundamental basis of the crisis, it made rather general recommendations with a view to their general application in the different countries which the group visited. In this respect it differed from the report of the East and Central Africa group which made a clear analysis of the situation obtaining in each country and gave definite recommendations. However, the West African report showed a depth of understanding of the issues involved by broadly stating that the aim of education is to enable the child to grow to the full stature of a man, sound in mind and body. The child should acquire all the necessary skills according to his ability to enable himself to be useful to himself and to his community. In other words, education is a preparation for life so that the child can effectively take his place in society. It is the means by which the human species hands its acquired experience and knowledge from one generation to another. Education is also an instrument of change, preparing people for any necessary adjustment to new social and political forms or a new environment. Education should help in giving the power for the discerning of truth. The supreme task of education in Africa is to discover the means by which the bad may be transformed into the good.

With regard to the problem of the organization of education on the West Coast, the group seemed to confirm the 'pyramid' system as an inevitable policy for education organization. Under this system everybody receives a basic education, but the numbers who reach each successive level after that become progressively smaller with only about .05% of those who started reaching university level.[7]

East and Central Africa Study Group

Throughout the report of the East and Central Africa group, great emphasis was laid on the vital value of the spiritual basis of education. Education, according to this group, must be rooted in a strong spiritual environment. Christian missions are encouraged to share the task of providing education for African people. The group

recorded its tribute to, and made an appraisal of, the role of missionaries in education. However, the report raised two points of some
importance in relation to the continued participation of missions in
education. First, the role of the Western missionary must not be that
of entrenching himself but rather of 'working himself out of the
job', to give greater responsibility to the African leadership. Secondly,
missionaries must not expect to be given control of education. Education is a public social service which is the responsibility of the state
and which, in consequence, the state must also control. The group
also pointed out that one of the disadvantages of missions engaging
in education is that denominational rivalry may be an obstacle to the
smooth organization of the system. In general the group admitted
that there was a strong anti-missionary feeling concerning their
future role in the educational system.

The group confirmed the existence of an intense desire for education
which could only be ignored at a great risk of disorder and degeneration in African society. There was also recognition of the importance of
education in helping to solve the enormous economic problems which
Africa faces. In the group's view, the vicious circle can only be
broken with a large supply of good teachers. In conclusion the group
recommended two steps in the organization of education : first, the
introduction of legislation to control the opening of private schools
and to ensure efficiency; secondly, the alteration of school systems
to provide for four years' primary education followed by a four
years' middle school course, and then four years' secondary school
course (the 4-4-4 system).[8]

General Report of the Cambridge Conference on African Education

The Report of the Cambridge Conference on African Education is
divided into five sections which represent the number of discussion
groups, each of which worked independently, all submitting their
findings to the plenary sessions of the Conference : Group A studies
Responsibility and Control of Education; Group B, The Expansion
of Educational Systems; Group C, The Teaching Profession; Group
D, Organization and the Curriculum; Group E, Education and the
Adult. A summary of the fundamental points raised and conclusions
is given below.

The group declared that 'there comes a time in the development of a nation and of its educational system when the nation assumes responsibility for the control of education'.[9] This time, in the group's view, had already arrived. Expansion of the educational system was dictated by the popular demand for education which, if not met, would result in chaos and degeneration. This would be the inevitable consequence of a lackof response on the part of the government and Christian missions. This conviction led the group to formulate five general principles which must underlie the plans for the expansion of education : (i) greater efforts must be made to make up the leeway in girls' education; (ii) the standards of secondary education and of teacher-training must not be neglected through too great a concentration on expanding the primary school system; (iii) primary school wastage must be stopped; (iv) a sufficient number of men and women of the right type must be attracted to the teaching profession and must be given the right sort of training and guidance; (v) primary education must be largely financed out of local education rates.

Of particular significance in this section of the report was the consideration of the place of the teacher in society and his role in public affairs. This is important because in the African communities there are few specialists and potential leadership is scarce. The teacher is often the only educated man in his community and must therefore take leadership seriously. The group courageously went further and ventured to open the contentious question of the teachers' participation in nation-building through party politics. It stated in no uncertain terms that :

> If a teacher wishes to enter central politics, he should be encouraged to do so, but it will not usually be possible for him to carry on his professional career while a member of the central legislature. In this case he should be given leave without pay while engaged in public life, and if he wishes to re-enter active teaching, he should be able to do so without losing his acquired rights. He must, of course, keep party politics out of the class room.[10]

This was an outlook that was welcome because of the legalistic attitude of many educational authorities on the matter.

The group also discussed the matter of professional standards and suggested ways in which these could be achieved, for example, by the establishment of a unified teaching service, teachers' associations, refresher courses, professional committees and summer schools. The importance of curriculum planning was emphasized and the conference maintained that this must essentially be related to the corresponding stages of the natural growth of the child. It was also agreed that attention should be paid to the need for moral and character training. The conference considered that the form of education which is provided for the adult must not be neglected. Adult education presents opportunities for the education of the adult at many levels and all should be given their place.

From all these studies it becomes clear that during the colonial period, and in spite of the many efforts made to achieve balance and progress in popular education, there was always disparity between the stated goals and plans of education, and what was actually achieved in the field. Many short and long term plans for educational expansion only increased frustration. The underlying reasons for this were that educational planning had little relation to the African conditions and African life; that although education had ceased to be regarded as a philanthropic service, it was still considered as a means to an end: the production of junior civil servants and, in the case of missions, the strengthening of church membership. Alternatively, education was considered as just one more of the public social services and not as an important process of human and social development; educational planning was done for, instead of with the African, who was not consulted about his needs. Even at the time of the Cambridge Conference, there were very few Africans in positions of responsibility and authority to be able to influence decisions and plans. However, in fairness to the conference, it must be stated that it had taken a courageous step forward in this direction. It was the most representative conference on African education and a small number of responsible African nationals had participated. This judgment is only in contrast with the Addis Ababa Conference on the Development of Education in Africa in 1961 which heralded a new era in the history of education in Africa. To some extent the Cambridge Conference seems to have anticipated the Addis Ababa Conference, as can be seen by the prophetic declaration of its chairman :

The next step which ought to succeed the Cambridge Conference

must inevitably take place in Africa. It is in the territories themselves that policies must be framed, their cost calculated and provided for, and the understanding and co-operation of organizations
sought and secured.[11]

The period between the Cambridge Conference and the Addis Ababa
Conference was a time of strenuous effort to interpret policy in action.
Great progress was made in many countries towards the provision
of popular education, but the problem of providing education to meet
the popular demand had to contend with the complications of social
and political changes such as the population movement from villages
into the few already overcrowded towns and cities, the general
increase in population and the lack of sufficient money. Consequent
upon independence, many countries had become disillusioned about
the whole basis of education and it was becoming clear that the
situation was getting out of hand. It was also clear that no one
country could tackle the problem on a large enough scale to meet
the challenge it presented. The solution lay in looking at the problem on a continental level and in appealing to agencies outside Africa.

NOTES

1. Lord Hailey, *An African Survey*, Oxford University Press 1956, p. 239.
2. Ibid., p. 1187.
3. Notes taken from the original Report of the Phelps-Stokes Fund, *Education in Africa: A Study of West, South and Equatorial Africa by the Education
Commission*, 1922, with the personal permission of Dr Patterson, President
of the Foundation, in the New York office.
4. Ibid., p. 1.
5. Ibid., p. 43.
6. *Cambridge Report on African Education*, 1953, p. 5.
7. Ibid., p. 12.
8. Ibid., p. 74.
9. Ibid., p. 143.
10. Ibid., p. 158.
11. Ibid., p. 183.

3

Education and the Process of Nation-building

An understanding of some of the factors which have influenced the evolution of the nations of Africa is of importance in order to see Africa in its proper perspective in world history. For this it is not necessary to go into a detailed study of the history of Africa before the Berlin Convention of 1885. This convention was the first international meeting specially called to discuss problems in Africa resulting from territorial occupation by Western powers and aimed to settle the quarrels which had arisen among colonial powers over the domains each was claiming.

The decisions of the convention, which involved drawing boundaries across outline maps of Africa, separated many hitherto homogeneous groups of people who now had to begin to regard themselves as a colonial people of one or the other of the Western colonial powers. The convention did not say much about the future of the peoples of these territories, but rather concerned itself with the arguments on territorial possessions and demarcation. In this connection Lord Hailey suggests that if there was any idea of self-determination for the native peoples, it was then only embryonic. He bases this remark on a statement in the Berlin Treaty that one of the many objectives of the settlement was 'the furthering of the moral and material well-being of the native peoples'.[1]

It will therefore be understood why so little progress was made in the changing of the attitude of colonial powers to their possessions in Africa. To put this in historical perspective we may point out that in the period between 1885, the year in which the Berlin

Convention was held, and 1950, which is a point at which the phenomenal social and political changes begin to show different manifestations, there were only two fully independent sovereign states in the whole sub-continent – Ethiopia and Liberia. Whereas these sixty-five years of colonial history were years of stagnation, the period between 1950 and 1960 saw the emergence of no less than twenty more independent states in a process that confounded any previous predictions. In these ten years the African Revolution had achieved what colonial history had failed to do in half a century, probably because it did not intend to do so.

The result of this has been that many African nations have received their independence with little or no preparation for the enormous task of welding together the fragmented groups, ethnic, tribal and racial, into single nations. The most harassing problem has been that of lack of leadership. To cite one instance, 'The new multi-racial Lovanium University near Kinshasa in the Congo Republic graduated its first Africans – seven of them – in 1958, but the New State University at Lubumbashi had not produced its first graduates by independence. Although 136 able "medical assistants" had completed training by independence, the first Congolese MD was not graduated from Lovanium University until 1961, and no Congolese had been educated as a lawyer during the entire period.'[2] There was in this case, at independence and before, a general shortage of professional and skilled workers. To quote another example of this shortage and of the seriousness of the crisis from the same book: 'When the great push came in 1959 to move Congolese civil servants up the ladder more rapidly and train them for the monumental task ahead, the government had to comb the junior public service to find 500 Africans for promotion to middle positions. Relatively few of the 500 had a secondary education.'

The situation in the Congo may be an extreme case, but the majority of African countries have had to start with such a handicap on their road to nationhood. In their efforts to rise to the situation, many have had to devise makeshift ways to meet the crisis. Leaders have had to be produced in a terrible hurry, often at the expense of efficiency. Everywhere the cry has been for education on a very large scale. Consequently, there have arisen crash programmes of educational development, emergency teacher training, airlifts of students to European countries, often without much regard to where the students might be trained and what type of training they might get. Many schemes, including imaginative economic plans, sometimes have to wait even when money is available, because of lack of suitable manpower – technicians, economists, accountants, teachers, doctors, nurses, lawyers, all have to be found and found quickly. A breakthrough is possible only with massive schemes of educational development. This crisis is even more serious than that described in the previous chapter, where the education system fell far too short of expectations. The situation is grave because of the expectations of all who have looked and worked for independence and to whom politicians made many promises and pledges, for example, for more education, better houses, and general economic prosperity.

An International Perspective

The other side of the crisis is related to the orientation and objectives of the present systems of education. The concept of education as the development of the whole man in relation to the community is being questioned because it lacks precise definition. The independent nations wish to make their educational policy clear in such a way that it will be directly related to the development of the nation. They want education to enable the individual to make a maximum contribution to national development. In one sense this is a reversal of the order of priorities. Instead of education being seen as for the good of the individual so that he can make a contribution to the community, it is being seen as a means to enable the individual to develop for the good of the community and therefore for himself. To be precise, new nations in Africa see education in relation to economic development. Education stands at the very centre of nation-building, in its economic development, in the business of social planning and in the development of political institutions. The question is how to bring this policy to realization. At the second Conference of Independent African States meeting in June, 1960, at Addis Ababa, a resolution was passed setting up the Council for Educational, Cultural and Scientific Co-operation in Africa. Among the tasks this council was charged to undertake was that of calling a meeting of experts in the field for the purpose of charting out the new course of educational, cultural and scientific development in Africa at a continental level.

In May 1961 a Conference of African States on the Development of Education in Africa was called, sponsored by the United Nations Educational, Scientific and Cultural Organization and the Economic Commission for Africa. This was the first international conference on education to be called in Africa by the African countries themselves, just as was predicted by Sir Philip Morris, Chairman of the Cambridge Conference on African Education in 1952.[3]

Review of the Addis Ababa Report on African Educational Development

Analysis of the report of the Addis Ababa Conference is necessary if we are to understand some of the new educational ideas and the current trend in the philosophy of education in Africa. It will give us some idea of the seriousness of the situation in education and the difficulties that must be overcome if there is to be a good climate for effective educational and national development plans.

Briefly, the origin of the conference was in the decision of the General Conference of UNESCO taken at its eleventh session 'to convene a conference of African States in 1961 with a view to establishing an inventory of educational needs and a programme to meet those needs in the coming years, and to invite the United Nations, the other Specialized Agencies and the International Atomic Energy Commission to co-operate with UNESCO in the preparation and organization of the Conference'.[4] This conference brought together government delegates and observers, United Nations agencies and international non-governmental organizations.

The purpose of the conference was stated to be 'to provide a forum for African States to decide on their priority educational needs, to promote economic and social developments in Africa and to establish tentative short-term and long-term plans for educational development ...' The conference decided that its immediate task was to establish 'quantitative and qualitative educational goals and targets both for a short period, 1961-1966, and a long period, 1961-1980'.[5] The problems in the following areas were considered: (i) Development of education in relation to African cultural and socio-cultural factors; (ii) Inventory of educational needs for economic and social developments; (iii) Education as a basic factor in economic and social development; (iv) Patterns of international co-operation for the promotion and implementation of the programmes of educational development.

The report also contains the 'Outline of a Plan for African Educational Development' which the conference approved unanimously. This outline plan is 'a synthesis of the educational demands, goals, targets and anticipated quantitative attainments during the next twenty years'.[6]

In contrast with the Cambridge Report on African Education which we studied in the previous chapter, the Report of the Conference of African States on the Development of Education in Africa is a rather businesslike document. It is a compendium of facts and figures on the problems of education and the possible ways of solving them. The impression one gains from the study of this report is that those who met to consider the numerous and complex problems of educational development in Africa must have been so certain about what they wanted that considerations of matters of theory seemed to be superfluous. The problems are dealt with in a precise and technical manner. Each paragraph is packed with facts stated in a way that leaves one in no doubt of the authority and status of the conference and those who constituted it. A few of the relevant issues which the conference sought to interpret in relation to the three ideas which have already been outlined will now be discussed in order to show the spirit and direction of the conference.

Education as a basis for social and national development

Among the items outlined in the inventory of educational needs is one concerned with the task of the re-orientation of African education to the cultural setting. 'The desire to accelerate the re-orientation of the educational patterns and systems to interpret them in terms of the economic and social needs of their individual areas' was a second major aspect. The African leaders wished to give proper stress in education at all levels and by all possible means to their own culture. As the students of Africa are exposed to the scientific and cultural influences of the outside world, they need to be thoroughly grounded in the knowledge of their own cultural heritage. The education for the future citizens of Africa must be a modern African education.[7]

We have already referred in chapter 2 to the evolution of the concept of the cultural value of education. As early as 1922 the Phelps-Stokes Commission drew the attention of all those concerned with educational policy in tropical Africa to the need to set education within the cultural environment of the child. The Cambridge Report echoed this challenge. There is evidence that attempts were made to introduce into the curriculum many elements and activities of African life. African songs and dances were encouraged and African handicrafts introduced. Emphasis in history was put on the history of Africa, including the study of its ancient empires and cultures. The basic problem seems to have been one of selecting those elements of African life and culture which are good and which make for progress rather than hinder it. The norm for this selection has always been in relation to Western culture or according to Christian standards of compatibility. In other words, people from outside the culture have been the judges of what is good and what is bad in African culture. This may well be at the root of the prevalent misunderstanding and disrespect for the cultures of Africa.

Cultural development

The renewed call by Africans themselves for the establishment of a cultural basis to education is essentially different from that which was made in the previous decades of educational development. Africans are not interested in a mere adaptation of a few useful elements from African life, but in the whole orientation of education in relation to intrinsic African values to make it African and not merely a useful instrument of power borrowed from Europeans. This desire to bring educational development into harmony with African culture should not raise fears of stagnation. African culture itself is not static, but has undergone several phases of change. Like other cultures it is exposed to external influences, it is dynamic and ready to draw upon the great repository of world cultures, especially Western culture. Education has to be brought into the central position of cultural development because it lends to it the element of progress. For this reason the leaders at the Addis Ababa Conference were convinced that 'if it is to fulfil its many functions satisfactorily, education in Africa must be African, that is, it must rest on a foundation of a specifically African culture and be based on special requirements of African progress in all fields'.[8]

In general the essence of this argument is that the present type of education tends to uproot the African child by bringing pressures upon him to accumulate knowledge which does not immediately relate to the life which he lives. Education fails when it does not make the child understand himself and his social and cultural past and the life of the society of which he is a member. It does not even help him to adjust himself intelligently to the changes in this society because he has no roots in his culture. He can only copy blindly those elements in Western culture which appear novel and attractive even if they do not help him to live effectively.

The ultimate end of the educational process, according to the new philosophy of the African society, is the unfolding of the 'African Personality'. The general criticism of the content and methods of the present system of education was that these were not in line with existing conditions, and were out of step with the demands of political independence, unrelated to the realities of the technical coming-of-age of many new African industrial societies, and unrelated also to the imperative process of economic development. The effect of this on the child is that it allows no room for his intelligence, powers of observation and creative imagination to develop freely in order to help him find his bearings in the world. The directive of the conference enjoins that: 'African educational authorities should revise and reform the content of education in the areas of curricula, textbooks and methods, so as to take account of the African environment, child development, cultural heritage and the demands of technological progress and economic development, especially industrialization ...'[9] The members of the conference also seem to have recognized the importance of seeing this development in relation to the universal culture and values. In consequence of this, they make a plea for the need to change certain traditional attitudes. The plea is for the educators of the African child to begin to think in global terms in order that African education may keep in step with the most recent developments and results of educational research. While insistence is on creating effective educational systems, attention is also drawn to the adaptation of methods and the production of textbooks, which must be in close relation with the child's cultural environment. Education in Africa will be good education only if it enables the African child to pass through the transition from the world of tribal control and influence to the world of nuclear science and the exploration of outer space. The world of primitive living is passing and the industrial communities, though numerically small, are making an irresistible impact on the old tribal structures. This, of course, creates problems for the new communities who move out of the natural securities of tribal society. New forms of social and psychological security have to be found. Education is an important element in the creation of a feeling of security.

Another problem inseparably connected with the development of culture in Africa is that of language. This is a very serious problem where education is being considered, and educational planning and research must take account of it. The kind of culture the Addis Ababa Conference talks about is a common culture of Africa. Culture can only be spread through contact and communication. The problem of contact is not insurmountable because territorial doors can be opened so that people, especially students, can move freely from one country to another for mutual benefit. The problem of communication, however, is real and complex, as the multiplicity of languages and the lack of an African *lingua franca* reduce the chances of the development of a common African culture. There are at present three European languages widely used in Africa – English, French and Portuguese. Of these three, Portuguese will eventually disappear and will not develop into a widely spoken language. English and French will continue to meet the present needs. However, foreign languages are not good vehicles for developing an intrinsically African culture. They are the languages of the *élite* and of those who have spent a reasonable number of years in school; the masses of the villages and towns cannot use them. There is therefore a great need for at least three common African languages for the communication of ideas from one country to another, in addition to the two European languages. This is an enormous problem which requires serious study and research. The Addis Ababa Conference was not very helpful here. If education has to help the child to be rooted in his culture, it will fail unless it gives him the necessary equipment to do this. The educational system in Africa must be designed to produce an African child who can live in three worlds; he must be rooted in his immediate culture and mother tongue, he must be able to find his way in the new all-African culture and at the same time be in touch with developments in the world at large.

Education, understood in general terms, is an important instrument for the transmission of culture and the general heritage of societies and communities. It has already been pointed out in a previous chapter that a simple kind of education had been going on in African tribal society for centuries and that by means of this process the experience of one generation was passed on to the next. African States are committed to a double objective in their future educational policy: (1) Education must help to modernize African society and give it dynamism and resourcefulness so that it is not out of step with contemporary modern societies; (2) Education must help to conserve and to rehabilitate African culture in such a way that it will be worthy of respect by other nations. There must be deliberate and planned social education to enable the child to acquire socially desirable values. This is the social role of education; to prepare the individual for effective and smooth entry into society as an adult.

With the break-up of the original primary groups in African societies, new social relations are coming into being. These are groups which, unlike the original tribal social groups, are not based on blood relationship and are no longer drawing for their cohesion on the common ancestral heritage. They are groups of modern technological Africans in which voluntarism is the major factor. Such a situation means that more than before the African child has to be helped to face the enormous problem of choice of his social group. The social role of education in Africa will therefore be, first, to prepare the African child to enter into the new societies that are coming into being, which have their basis in industrial and urban life, to live in them effectively and to contribute to these societies according to his ability and to the extent to which his social awareness has been aroused by preparation in school. Secondly, education should also sharpen the child's awareness of his cultural heritage and be a means by which this culture is revitalized. This process will form an important element in the school as an ideal African social system, in which the child will learn the business of living in changing social structures, and of accepting and discharging social and political responsibilities which his nation gives him. Education, then, must help the child to develop national consciousness.

So far we may have seemed to idealize the emerging societies. It must also be stated, however, that these contain many tensions and contradictions which are the birth-pangs of the new nations and new societies. All those concerned are agreed that the greatest need for the new African nations, if they are to make rapid and effective progress, is stability, particularly social stability, as this is a prerequisite for successful development in all aspects of national life. The function of education here should be to remove the ignorance which often lies at the root of tension and lack of mutual understanding of common national goals. A long and intelligent view of education should therefore take into account the fact that true education is that which helps to bring development in all aspects of human life. Economic development, though important, is only a small part of the whole. It is with this conviction that we shall endeavour to examine and to make some critical observation on the emphasis which leaders of African nations intend to give in their educational planning. In general, too much weight is being given to the technical aspects of education and not enough to the fundamental questions underlying the present pressure for a new evaluation of educational systems in Africa.

The seriousness of the need to relate educational planning to economic development is reflected in Professor Paul Mercier's address to the Conference of African States on Development of Education in Africa.[10] He emphasizes the social role of education by calling attention to the fact that a successful programme of development, including economic development, is dependent to a large extent upon a good understanding of the social and cultural environment and processes in the nation or society concerned. For this reason there must be serious research in this field in order that the programmes of development may operate in the context of a well-understood social background. This, of course, requires co-operation and mutual exchange of experiences relating to the formulation of policies which in turn will affect the process of economic development.

All these problems are now weighing upon the shoulders of the new African nations, and their statesmen will need to be constantly reminded of the necessary priorities in nation-building. To use William Paton's words, the burden is no longer the white man's. Self-determination and independence mean that the nations are mature enough to look after themselves, but international awareness in the last few years has fostered the desire for mutual co-operation in education. As has already been pointed out, the problems are too complex for each nation to attempt to solve in isolation. International co-operation, of course, means exposure to the opinion of the world and this may be a very healthy thing for the new nations which are susceptible to the dangers of petty and unprogressive self-centredness. Education is an invaluable corrective in this respect because it widens a people's outlook on life and the world. Educational needs are going to press the nations in Africa into a unity of purpose, as is exemplified by the Addis Ababa Conference.

Educational planning and economic development

The idea of the economic value of education is not new in Africa. In many territories it has been one of the principal features in the demand for popular education. This concept of education has arisen from a number of factors, among which is the desire to get away from tribal control and from its precarious subsistence economy. Of particular significance, however, is the colonial policy which looked at education as a source for filling the junior administrative jobs, thereby creating a white-collar job mentality. Education thus acquired a wrong meaning, and it is therefore not surprising that at a time when Africans have to decide what kind of education they want, present views on the subject should be expressed in such strong terms from men of the highest responsibility. Education has to be geared to plans for economic and social development and its value is therefore considered in relation to technical needs and programmes. Whereas for the Christian missions education was a means for evangelism and for the colonial administrator a means for introducing Western colonization, for the African it was important for its economic value and for its own sake, since knowledge is power. It was common throughout Africa for illiterate parents to make great sacrifices in order to promote the education of one gifted child, in the hope that this would pay handsome returns and also create more opportunities for the education of the other children; the principle of 'each one educate one' is a well known social and educational pattern. Sometimes members of an extended family[11] would syndicate their wealth to sponsor the educational career of one or more of the gifted youngsters. This was considered a good investment as well as a source of prestige for the family concerned.

At the highest level of this concept, economists contend that education is an important national investment. One of its effects on economic prosperity, they claim, is that by training the worker it is possible to increase his productive capacity in industry. Education awakens the mind of the worker and gives him sensitivity to the processes around him. It helps to increase his efficiency and removes sloppiness in methods of work. Even elementary education for a few years opens greater opportunities for advancement. In this connection A. Marshall, an eminent English economist, justifies expenditure of public or private funds on education as a profitable investment because it opens up opportunities for advancement to the masses who would otherwise be unable to bring to full use their latent abilities. Quite apart from this 'the economic value of one great industrial genius is sufficient to cover the expenses of the education of a whole town; for one new idea, such as Bessemer's chief invention,[12] adds as much to England's productive power as the labour of a hundred thousand men'.[13]

This seems to be more or less the motive behind the emphasis that the Conference of African States on Education gave to the economic significance of education, and there would seem to be every justification for such an objective. However, it is to be hoped that African educationists and economists will also heed the voice of sociologists concerning the social implications of the application of this philosophy, and that there will be careful study of the sociological processes involved. It could be that they will precipitate a moral reaction leading to instability in the nation, which may frustrate the expectation of material abundance.

This view is by no means confined to Africa; it is increasingly becoming clear that here is a consequence of the internationalization of education. Evidence of this is in the general international concern for the planning of educational development, as expressed in the formation of an international body. The International Institute for Educational Planning was established in July 1963 under the sponsorship of UNESCO, the World Bank and the Ford Foundation. The express purpose of this body was to bring educators and economists together to find ways in which educational planning could be made more effective by making maximum use of all resources, material and manpower, and by devising methods and curricula which would be closely related to, and in harmony with the economic and social needs of the countries concerned. The institute serves as a co-ordinating centre for educational planning and is ready to give advice to countries which are making plans for educational development. This institute also acts as a clearing house for educational assistance between countries, especially the developing countries of Africa. The main objective of the institute is to make education productive.

Economic basis of education

The Addis Ababa Report shows a bias towards the need for matching educational planning to rapid economic development. All states in Africa are urged to make their plans for educational expansion as part of the overall national development plan and to relate them to the programmes of national economic and social development. As has already been indicated, the report states in no uncertain terms that 'the purpose of the Conference was to provide a forum for African States to decide on their priority educational needs to promote economic and social development in Africa, and in the light of these, to establish first tentative short-term and long-term plans for educational development in the continent, embodying the priorities they had decided upon for the economic growth of the region'.[14] Further, the conference called for radical change in the direction and systems of education 'in order to meet new economic needs'. For this reason, the secondary level of education is to be given greater attention. It is at this level that education can be made economically productive as it increases the area of manpower resources. 'Targets indicated by many African States are impressive; for example, to double the secondary school intake in the next five years, to triple the secondary school intake by 1970.'[15]

An appraisal of this new approach to educational development in relation to nation-building is of importance if the spirit of the new nations and their aspirations are to be understood. Of particular interest is the way in which the conference made an evaluation of higher education in relation to the urgent need for the nations to develop the necessary manpower resources. In the inventory of educational needs over the next few years the conference has this to say about higher education :

> Facilities for higher education at the present time are far from adequate for the training of the necessary cadres of specialists, researchers, administrators and other leaders. For example, a manpower survey recently conducted in African states indicates that, despite drastic efforts at expansion of higher educational facilities and through training abroad, the need for men with academic and professional qualifications in the next five years would be in the region of 20,000 while the output of individuals trained locally and overseas in the same period was estimated at 3,000. To meet a similar need, the objective of another African state is to increase its university population from the present 1,000 to between 7,500 and 10,000 in the 1970s.[16]

This shows the odds against the new nations in their effort to meet manpower needs for the building of national structures. There is no other alternative, it appears, but to rely for the time being upon manpower resources from outside Africa, particularly for the staffing of the new universities and technological institutions. This situation calls for co-operative effort not only among the African states but also between Africa and the more developed countries of the world.

To return to the question of education and economics, the overall impression about this philosophy is that there were many issues to which the conference did not give the serious attention they deserve. However, the report indicates that the conference recognized that there were still many open questions. Chapter 2 of the report deals, among other things, with 'Education as a Productive Investment'. In this connection the conference recognizes that 'Education does not have for its primary purpose a greater production of goods and services', but that 'Education would therefore have value even if it contributed nothing to economic development'.[17] In other words, what makes one see education in relation to economic development is the fact that it is development that absorbs a good part of the national revenue.

All the foregoing facts and problems are further analysed in the supplementary report called 'Outline of a Plan for African Educational Development'. This is the result of an agreement reached by the African States in the conference. It embodies a five year plan as a first step in educational development with a further twenty year plan for African educational development for the countries of tropical Africa. It is a plan of educational objectives and priorities, an attempt to make estimates of capital requirements to underwrite these plans as well as to make an assessment of current expenses, and to take into account rates of population increase. In the following discussion of this outline plan some problems at the different levels of education, that is from primary school to university, will be examined.

NOTES

1. Lord Hailey, *An African Survey*, p. 239.
2. Ruth C. Sloan, *The Educated African*, p. 194.
3. Cambridge Report on African Education, Chapter II.
4. Final Report of the Conference of African States on the Development of Education in Africa, ECA/UNESCO, 1961, p. v.
5. Ibid., pp. v and vi.
6. Ibid., p. vi.
7. Ibid., p. 3.
8. Ibid., p. 55.
9. Ibid., p. 23.
10. Ibid., pp. 81-96.
11. The extended family is a kinship system which includes members beyond the basic family unit of father, mother and children.
12. Bessemer's process of forcing air into molten pig iron to drive out impurities revolutionized industry.
13. Alfred Marshall, *Principles of Economics*, 1962, p. 179.
14. Report of the Conference of African States on Education, p. v.
15. Ibid., p. 5.
16. Ibid., p. 6.
17. Ibid., p. 9.

4

The Strategy of Educational Planning in Relation to Nation-building

So far we have discussed the ideal place of education in nation-building and have agreed that education is or should be at the centre of any effective process of national development. We shall now turn to a discussion of the actual situation and how the problems of educational expansion are being tackled. This involves a discussion of the strategy of educational development and expansion in relation to the needs of the countries of Africa, and the means at their disposal. The Plan for African Educational Development, the report of which is related to the General Conference of African States on the Development of Education in Africa, outlines proposals to form the basis for meeting educational needs. A discussion of some of the general principles which underlie the strategy of educational planning will be useful here. The second part of this chapter is concerned with an analysis of this plan and with a discussion of the place of the churches in education in Africa.

Some important considerations in educational planning

The basic strategy of educational planning is broadly speaking 'sensitivity'. The planners must always be sensitive to the needs and opinions of the country and be aware of the means available to implement the plans to be made, so as to ensure that no mystery surrounds the plan, but that it becomes the plan of the nation. There should also be some estimation of the results which will be produced under normal social, political and economic conditions, assum-

ing, of course, that the plan is followed faithfully. In order that
there should be no mystery surrounding the plan, two points should
be considered: first, the plan should include as many people as
possible, and planners must be willing to listen to all kinds of com-
plaints and misgivings; secondly, the plan should be as simple as it
is possible to make it so that it can be explained to people not only
in the towns but also in the villages. This is why there cannot be
a standard or universal educational plan. The needs, conditions and
means of each situation must be considered in a particular plan. On
the other hand, it is possible to have a model educational plan or
broad outline to provide some basis for national plans. For this
reason the Addis Ababa Plan is rightly conceived as a broad outline
and not as a master plan which must be used by every country
without due regard to local conditions and needs.

Here are some needs which an educational plan must try to meet.
Needs differ according to the conditions, historical circumstances,
culture and level of development of each country, but African nations
today share a common need for trained men and women to man
their gigantic development plans; they need teachers, doctors, nurses,
lawyers, economists, agriculturalists, technicians and skilled artisans.
They need hundreds of thousands of trained men and women in all
of these categories. The urgency of the need for trained personnel
of all kinds arises from the realization that modern nation-building
is a complex process which requires men with specialized training
in many fields. The strategy here, then, is to make an assessment of
the manpower requirements of the country concerned in order to
see areas in which there are serious gaps. This assessment naturally
affects educational plans and the content of education as well as the
emphasis and priorities of the educational system. One country may
experience greatest need for manpower resources in order to develop
and exploit its natural resources. Such need might be felt because
of the desire to develop a country's agricultural potentials; or
because of the construction and development of a national communi-
cations network; or in the development of utility services such as
electricity and irrigation. Other countries may feel greater need for
the professional services – administration, industrial management and
commerce. These needs are not peculiar to any one country, but the
priorities in each country will differ according to the greatest need

and the resources available.

Few of the nations in Africa have made a thorough survey of their manpower needs. A preliminary survey of high level manpower potentialities and resources gives a disturbing picture; it shows, for instance, that with all the efforts a country can make, it cannot meet all its manpower needs without large recruitment from outside. A commission which investigated the future needs for post-secondary and higher education in Nigeria[1] seems to confirm what in general is the experience of many countries in Africa. That is, that only one-sixth to one-third of the population has appropriate educational qualifications for the number of jobs for which a general secondary education is the minimum.

The consequence of this situation is an enormous gap between demand and supply of manpower and it emphasizes the importance of giving secondary education special attention. The greater part of the process of nation-building will be in the expansion of services of all kinds and in industrial development including agriculture. The greatest need for manpower, therefore, will be in the middle and lower categories of personnel. A country will effect greatest saving in the long run if it rationalizes deployment of resources for educational expansion by investing them in secondary education and by recruiting high-level personnel from outside to teach in secondary vocational schools and technical colleges. This policy would pay higher dividends than the recruitment of expatriate technicians, artisans and people in the lower professions, since a country can only afford to bring in a limited number of them, and they would in fact be doing what can be done by the local population. This is not a very attractive proposition since it is likely to slow down development and productivity, but once the flow of skilled men begins, it will more than compensate for the leeway caused by the period of training.

The Addis Ababa Conference considered manpower assessment as an important first step in the planning of educational expansion. To this end the conference recommended :

the establishment within a single Ministry or in a form of inter-ministerial commission, of manpower boards with the following functions; assessment of present manpower resources and needs both in the public and private sector, long-range forecasting of manpower requirements, development of programmes for education and training of manpower, including on the job training of employed manpower; formulation of policy governing the importation of high-level manpower from abroad; development of programmes to alleviate unemployment or underemployment; formulation of social security measures in relation to the national plans for economic and social development; study of incentives including the setting of wages and salaries and of the effect upon the allocation and effective utilization of manpower.[2]

Many countries have now established manpower boards or committees, others have erected manpower and training departments within the machinery of government administration. These are related to programmes of staff development and localization. The question of manpower in relation to nation-building will be discussed in chapter seven.

Another educational need which has to do with the process of nation-building is that of creating an intelligent and responsible citizenry. This is one of the general national aims of educational development, although there are dangers of abuse of this ideal if education becomes too nation-centred without due regard to the individual for whom the system is designed. However, national expenditure on education can be justified on these grounds alone, that is, if it is directed towards the production of well-informed and responsible individuals, because these will be a source of strength and stability to the nation. The new nations in Africa will spare no effort to help their people to move from a state of ignorance and illiteracy to a state of enlightenment. This would certainly help in closing the gap which still exists between the highly educated and the illiterate masses and would increase the number of those who can actively and intelligently participate in the work of building the new national structures. To this end one of the results hoped for from the education plan is the creation of an enlightened group which, for lack of a better term, may be called a middle class. The absence of a middle class in many countries in Africa is a serious gap, as a vigorous and well-informed middle class can be an important and effective corrective, especially under the African one-party systems of political development. Moreover, the presence of an enterprising middle class is generally taken as a sign of national and economic vitality.

Each level of educational development, primary, secondary and higher, has its important claim in the plans for expansion. A good national education plan will not overlook these claims. It will recognize that a country's needs are many and that, although all are important, no one country, developed or under-developed, has yet reached a stage where it can meet all of them. A good educational plan should convince people that, among the many things that are wanted, there are needs which are so urgent and vital for the development of the country that neglect of these claims would cause difficulties in development. New nations for whom independence held out great hopes, often greater than their resources justified, will need to have this brought home to them gently and firmly. This means that the plan will need to work out priorities. It also means that while in some countries people will have to wait for the introduction of universal primary education, in others it will mean that they will have to wait for the highly-prized national status symbol – the university – in favour of the expansion and improvement of the secondary level of education.

In the past, political groups before and soon after independence have laid emphasis on the expansion of the primary level of education. For them it is a good political strategy to have an enlightened electorate and at the primary level it is possible to bring about a spectacular change. Yet it must also be said that expansion in primary education has not always come from political pressure alone, but especially from the unprecedented demand of parents for education. There is, however, another new factor in this pressure for popular education. The practical responsibilities for nation-building and economic development demand the production of men and women with more than primary school education – hence the new emphasis on the expansion of secondary school education. In support of this idea, the International Labour Organization holds the conviction that 'A solid foundation of general education at as advanced as possible a level provides a basis for acquiring vocational specialization and facilitates structural changes in the economy.'[3]

Educational plans will need to take account of the enormous problems created by the expansion of primary education in the last ten or fifteen years. In the first place, planning must remedy some, although not all, of the mistakes of this pressured expansion. Secondly, the new emphasis on the expansion of secondary education should not blind those who have to make plans to the lessons of the past, such as the shortage of teachers, classrooms, accommodation, lowering of standards consequent on large classes, and the over-production of an inadequately equipped youth who only add to the already big problem of unemployment. It is also true that at the secondary level of education, one is far better equipped to be able to advance rapidly when given further training through vocational and technical schools or by in-service training. Even here, however, there are still many dangers of an over-emphasis which may lead to over-production in a few fields at the expense of other important aspects of national development.

A total expansion of secondary education would bring problems out of proportion to the resources now available within Africa. The Addis Ababa Conference has made an estimate of the necessary requirements to meet the demands both for the short and long-term plans. The short-term plan covers the period 1961-6 and the long-term 1961-81. Even for the short term, the needs are enormous. At the end of each of these plans, namely 1966 and 1981, the position at all levels of education would be as shown in Table I. In this table it was assumed that in 1966 50% of the population of school age would be enrolled and in 1981 100%; that the teacher-pupil ratio at the primary level would be 1:45 in 1966 and 1:35 in 1981, allowing for replacement and increase of teachers in relation to the normal increase in enrolment. In addition, account was taken of the need for effective supervision of schools, which would require a large force of inspectors or supervisors. It is estimated that for effective supervision there should be one inspector for every 5,000 pupils. At the secondary school level it was also assumed that the pupil-teacher ratio would be 1:20 in 1966 and 1:19 in 1981, and that the total secondary school enrolment would be 12% and 18% of the total primary school enrolment for 1966 and 1981 respectively. The total cost of education at the end of each of these plans is estimated at 1,154.4 million dollars in 1966 and 2,593.4 million dollars in 1981.

TABLE I[4] :   The position as at the end of the two plans

Level of Education	Position at 1966 (Short-term)	Position at 1981 (Long-term)
1 Primary Education		
Estimated school age population	29,831,000	32,808,000
Estimated enrolment	15,279,000	32,808,000
Total number of teachers	383,300	1,014,100
2 Secondary Education		
(a) General secondary education	1,320,100	3,986,000
(b) Technical and vocational	334,100	1,547,400
(c) Teacher training	179,300	372,000
Total number of teachers	113,000	336,300
3 Higher Education		
Estimated enrolment in Africa	14,300	296,000
Estimated enrolment in other countries	16,000	32,000
Total enrolment	30,300	328,000

Looking at these proposals now, in the year 1970, we see that although much has been done to reach these targets, many countries have not achieved their goals.

An outline of a plan for African educational development

The outline plan for African educational development is an attempt to put into action strong convictions about the realistic ways in which the continuing crisis in African education can be averted. The present situation cannot be allowed to go on even for a few more years, as it threatens the very basis of the development of the new nations. A situation where the average proportion of children of school age who can be provided for in the present schools is 16%, and in some cases as low as 2%, can only be regarded as serious. African states have therefore declared their determination to close this gap as fast as their resources and other important considerations make it possible. If they are not to make more mistakes, and therefore make the situation even more complicated, careful plans must be made. As the situation dictates that such plans must be on a vast scale, co-operation among the states is absolutely necessary, and since the resources necessary also have to be on a very large scale, African nations must appeal to other nations outside Africa. Lack of economic development is one of the major causes of shortage of resources. With their meagre funds, 'some African governments are now committing to the development of education up to 23% of their national budgets'.[5] A typical example of the important place of education in national planning is that of Sierra Leone with its ten-year development plan in which education accounts for more than 29 million dollars or more than 10% of the total capital cost of 278 million dollars. The sum allocated was to be spent during the first five years of the plan.[6] Similarly, Zambia allocated nearly 55 million out of a total of over 395 million dollars to education in its first national development plan. But this is not enough, so that African states have appealed for international assistance also. Half-measures are hopeless in this situation, as they would only bring more frustration. If there is to be a spectacular change, many times more children than the present enrolment must be enabled to attend school. This, in practice, means the construction of a vast number of schools and provision of other educational facilities and services on a scale never before undertaken in Africa.

The Outline Plan surveys the needs to be met if educational expansion as envisaged by the Addis Ababa Conference is to be carried out effectively. The areas and problems which call for immediate attention are finances, materials, teachers, curriculum reform, education of girls, higher education, adult education and planning. Thus, for instance, in curriculum reform the plan makes a strong plea for improvement in the content of textbooks used in African schools and emphasizes the need for writing new ones which will take into account the African environment and cultural background. Further, the plan sets out the basis on which priorities in education are to be determined. A need is given the status of 'priority' when it is basic to the development of a balanced educational programme and is directly related to accelerated economic and social growth. On this basis the conference decided on the following priorities: secondary education; curriculum reform; teacher training, and directed that educational development planning must pay attention to

these. The following tables show the development at the different
levels of education and the relative cost of this expansion.

TABLE II: Short-term Plan (1961-6) Enrolment and Costs[7]

Level	1960-1	1961-2	1962-3	1963-4	1964-5	1965-6
	Enrolment (in thousands)					
Primary	11,187.0	11,586.0	12,203.0	13,028.0	14,050.0	15,279.0
Secondary	816.6	903.7	1,025.0	1,224.7	1,475.2	1,833.5
Higher	25.0	25.5	26.2	27.2	28.5	30.3
Total cost in millions of dollars		584.4	654.0	821.4	941.6	1,154.4

The short-term plan has already been implemented in many countries.
The characteristic of this period (1961-6) was accelerated development
and general experimentation. The long-term plan includes the period
of the short-term plan but takes a long view of the development of
education in anticipation of reaching the goals, e.g. universal primary
education, an efficient secondary level education and sufficient
facilities within Africa for full higher education.

TABLE III: Long-term Plan (1961-81) Enrolment and Costs[8]

Level	1961-2	1965-6	1970-1	1980-1
	Enrolment (in thousands)			
Primary	11,586.0	15,279.0	20,378.0	32,808.0
Secondary	903.7	1,833.5	3,390.0	5,905.4
Higher	25.5	30.3	55.0	328.0
Total cost in millions of dollars	584.4	1,154.4	1,881.6	2,593.4

Goals to be reached through the Short-term Plan

1. To increase the total school enrolment from 11 to 15 million.
2. To ensure the expansion of secondary education.
3. To provide greater enrolment in institutions of higher education and therefore promote advance in high-level manpower

training, and to provide increased enrolment for teacher-training on which primary educational expansion depends.

Some basic assumptions in the Outline Plans

(a) *Primary education* In the expansion of primary education the target is to increase enrolment annually by 5% of the intake. The recurrent cost per pupil is assumed to be 20 dollars per year; the cost of building 1,500 dollars per classroom for 50 pupils. 50% of the existing schools are to be equipped and school buildings improved within ten years.

(b) *Secondary education* The need calls for an output of 45,000 additional teachers each year and costing for teacher-training is based on the assumption that at least 50% of staff should be trained graduates.

Residence will be provided for all students and teachers and necessary costs per student will be 400 dollars at the lower stage and 600 dollars at the higher stage. Capital costs will be 1,000 dollars per pupil. Costs for other forms of secondary education are lower.

(c) *Higher education* The recurrent cost of each student at university in scientific and technical faculties in Africa is 1,600 dollars, as compared with 2,000 for each student studying abroad. Capital costs for building additional places at African universities are calculated at 10,000 dollars per place in scientific and technical faculties and at 5,000 dollars per place in other faculties and in non-university institutions.

Some of these outline plans have already been realized while others are still to be achieved. They could only be expected to be successful if educational, social, political and economic conditions were constantly normal.

Christian Education in Africa: Policy and Planning[9]

The Conference on Christian Education in Africa was held in January 1963 under the auspices of the All Africa Church Conference, a body through which a number of Protestant Churches in Africa plan for co-operation and common Christian action in all matters affecting the life of the church and nations in Africa. The conference was held in response to the challenge of the Addis Ababa meeting of African states on the development of education in Africa. This challenge arose from the new trend which the Addis Ababa Conference had shown of relating education to the needs of changing Africa, a trend to which the churches had not yet paid attention despite their long experience and involvement in education. In the second place, the challenge is implicit in the emphasis of the ministers of education on the importance of planning as a necessary first step in educational expansion.

The conference brought together a number of responsible and well-informed people in the field of education who have a special concern for the Christian basis of education. The main idea of the conference was to stimulate interest, to arouse a sense of concern among Christians and churches, and to make a fresh appraisal of their past and new relationships in the development of education. In the light of this appraisal, churches would make plans for Christian education, evaluate their role in the development of national systems of education and consider bases for international co-operation in dealing with problems of African educational expansion. This conference will be referred to as the Salisbury Conference, the name of the city where it took place.

The value of the Report of the Salisbury Conference is perhaps in providing a basic philosophy of education in Africa, if it is considered in relation to the more technical character of the Addis Ababa Report. This fact points to the special contribution which the churches are able to make to the process of educational development in Africa; namely that of providing the basic principles for this process and expansion. In their own evaluation of the significance of the conference, some of those who took part in its work have expressed their optimism with regard to the impact that it could make on the whole direction of Christian education and the Christian contribution. Its effect, it is hoped, might be felt in some similar way to that of the Phelps-Stokes Commission in 1924.

Some important considerations of the Salisbury Conference

(a) *The goals of Christian education*   Goals for Christian education are expressed in terms of the values which Christians wish to see enshrined in the national systems of education. Among these values are the following: 'The understanding of the world which has been created by God, the development of true relations with other persons and the means of communicating with them; the development of the talents God gives to each of us so that we may earn our daily bread and be of service to others; the capacity of awe and wonder, the capacity to make responsible decisions.'[10]

(b) *Responsibility for education* Christians and churches also see education as essential to nation-building, but they are aware of the dangers of this aim when it loses sight of the deeper dimensions of the life of the individual and the nation. The responsibility of the state for education is fully recognized, especially 'to help set and maintain standards of education at all levels, provide necessary professional supervision and ensure that provision is made for moral and religious instruction in the national systems of education. The responsibility of the church is the establishment of Christian schools to work within the national systems and to foster co-operation among churches and with the governments'.[11] The conference, however, recognized the fact that there was growing opposition in some countries against further participation of the church in education.

(c) *Policy and planning of Christian education* In the consideration of problems of policy and planning of Christian education, the conference had as a starting point an evaluation of the bases on which church participation in educational development could be justified. One of these is that of running good schools, staffed by teachers of high quality and calibre. Education should not be undertaken merely to maintain the prestige of the church, but also in order to make a contribution to the nation.

The principles for the planning of Christian education should include flexibility; quality rather than quantity; a broad-based service which extends beyond schools and colleges; and an emphasis on experimentation and pioneer work. Among the special areas of education to which churches are urged to pay particular attention are teacher-training, secondary and adult education and girls' education. Planning is of vital importance. Each church or Christian council must make its own plans and carry out constant study of the problems of education. The churches are also requested to help their governments to implement the recommendations of the Addis Ababa Conference. The conference considered all the effective ways of facing the new problems in African education and unanimously accepted the recommendation for establishing a Bureau of Christian Education within the structure of the All Africa Conference of Churches. The conference further specified the functions of this bureau as to:

(i) compile and exchange information about Christian education in the countries of Africa;

(ii) prepare statistics of areas of Christian educational effort in Africa;

(iii) assist Christian Councils in their educational planning;

(iv) maintain relationships with UNESCO and other international bodies;

(v) co-ordinate and stimulate external aid for Christian education in Africa from the churches and from educational trusts and foundations overseas;

(vi) supply information about, and co-ordinate, offers of scholarship assistance.

(d) *Priorities in educational planning*

(i) Teacher-training is given the highest priority because the whole fabric of education, from the point of view of the churches, depends upon the training of teachers who will lay the foundations.

(ii) Secondary education is the next area of priority as it is the basis for an adequate supply of personnel of high calibre.

(iii) The education of women, which in the past has suffered through neglect because of the conservative African traditional attitudes to the place of women in society, is important.

(iv) Adult education is important, for it is through this means that a literate and informed community can be established.

(e) *The content of education*   The underlying basis of the content of African education in general and of education in Christian schools in particular is knowledge of the background of the African child: the recognition of the intrinsic value of the social life of the community from which the child comes. The Salisbury Conference discussed in outline the emphasis which ought to be given in the teaching of all subjects, especially in the primary and secondary schools. In many respects the Salisbury Report confirms the Tananarive recommendations.[12] The Salisbury Conference dealt only with broad outlines, particularly in relation to the teaching of science, languages, history, geography and art.

A fact worthy of note in connection with the significance of the Conference of Churches on Christian Education is that UNESCO interests were represented, just as the interests of the churches were represented at the Conference of African States on the Development of Education in Africa. This is one of the significant signs of co-operation between the UNESCO interests concerned with African educational development and the All Africa Conference of Churches in the promotion of educational plans and advancement. The churches have still to make an even greater contribution, but need to realize that conditions have changed. This means that they will make their contribution in ways perhaps different from those of the past. The Salisbury Conference has gone a long way towards challenging the churches in Africa to undertake new responsibilities in the meeting of the educational needs of their nations. It has stimulated fresh thinking on the problems of educational expansion and has reiterated the need for maintaining sound Christian principles in the African systems of education.

NOTES

1. The Ashby Report of the Commission on Post-School Certificate and Higher Education in Nigeria, Federal Ministry of Education, Nigeria, Lagos 1960.

2. Final Report of the Conference of African States on the Development of Education in Africa, pp. 42-3.

3. ILO: Report of the Director-General, Programme and Structure of the ILO, 1962, p. 41.

4. Figures taken from the Outline of a Plan for African Educational Development, UNESCO 1961, in some cases arrived at by adding figures for appropriate items.

5. Ibid., p. 5.

6. *The New York Times*, 'Economic Review of an Emerging Africa', January 20, 1964.

7. Final Report of the Conference of African States on the Development of Education in Africa, ch. IV.

8. Ibid.

9. AACC: Report of the Conference on Christian Education in Changing Africa, OUP 1963.

10. Ibid., pp. 35-6.

11. Ibid., p. 43.

12. The Conference on the Adaptation of General Secondary School Curriculum in Africa, Tananarive, UNESCO 1962.

5

The Organization and Systems
of African Education

The popular description of the structure of education as it appears
in many territories in Africa is that of a 'pyramid'. At the base of
this pyramid are the primary schools in which the greater proportion
of the school age population is enrolled. Primary education lasts from
four to six years. About 20% of those at primary school should move
upward to the next level of the pyramid and be enrolled into secondary schools. The remainder of the primary population will have been
thinned out by selection and promotion and by the notorious
phenomenon of wastage, which in some countries is as high as 10%.
Similarly there is a small privileged *élite* at the top of the secondary
schools destined to higher forms of education in universities and
higher technical institutions. The Addis Ababa proposals confirm
this structure and, in fact, envisage the widening of the base by
introducing universal primary education. This, in turn, would boost
the level of secondary education. At present, however, the most
urgent need is for an expansion in secondary education in which
quality is maintained.

Each level of education has its valid claims on the resources of the
country. It is also true that all levels, primary, secondary and higher,
are interdependent, and that too much expansion in one may affect
the others adversely. This is one of the reasons why the implementation of the Addis Ababa proposal for African educational expansion
must be watched with great interest and concern.

The administration of and authority for education still varies from
country to country, but there is now a generally accepted principle

that the state is the final authority in the field. Through a ministry of education or some other similar statutory body the state maintains standards by providing supervision and sees to it that the necessary money is available for the operation of the system. In many territories, voluntary agencies continue to play an important role in the systems of education and, of these, the church is the most significant. In some countries churches have responsibility for as much as 50% of the national education, particularly in primary education. They generally receive financial support for their work from the state and Christian agencies outside and inside Africa. There are also local education authorities in a number of countries which help to bear the burden of education.

Each of these levels of education, primary, secondary and higher, will now be considered from the point of view of (1) basic assumptions and objectives, (2) content and alternative forms in levels where these apply, (3) prospects for the future. Methods of teaching will not be considered except in relation to a discussion of curriculum reform.

The primary level of education

Primary education in Africa is literally primary. There are few countries where any form of pre-school education exists, and the African child first comes into contact with organized formal education at the age of six or seven. In general, primary education in Africa cannot be considered on the same basis as that in Western countries as it has to fulfil two functions. It must, on the one hand, be a complete education in itself in order to provide a useful and significant education for the mass of children whose school career ends at this level. On the other hand, it has to prepare the comparatively small number of those who have to move on to secondary education. Often the primary school suffers in this attempt to achieve two ends and in many cases neither objective is accomplished satisfactorily. This situation is bound to remain and even be aggravated by the establishment of universal primary education. It might be argued that an improvement could be effected by giving particular attention to curriculum reform and the training of better teachers. The question, however, is not so simple because of the many pressures which are being brought to bear upon the schools. For example, many parents are demanding a type of primary education that may not be in harmony with their child's psychological and physiological development. There is also the pressure of political opinion, as 'education for all' is often the stock political promise.

The two functions which primary education in Africa is expected to fulfil must also be seen in relation to the length and age range of the course.

Length and age range of the primary school education

Primary education is differently organized in different African countries, but in general there are three basic systems:

(a) A six-year course in the age range of 6-12 years.
(b) A four-year course in the age range of 8-12 years.
(c) A four-year course in the age range of 5-9 years.

The basic assumptions underlying these arrangements are not very easy to explain. In some countries they are dictated by economic and social conditions. In tribal communities in which economic life requires the services of the child, the child will enrol late and must end his school career as soon as possible: hence the four-year course starting at eight and ending at twelve. The four-year course from five to nine years is dictated by the available national resources for education and the rationale is that it is best to give something, however inadequate, as quickly as possible and to as many people as possible. The six-year course works on the assumption that there is an age at which education can have a permanent value and that is somewhere between five and eleven years. There is the added advantage that selection for the secondary school course at the end of the twelfth year avoids the necessity of 'intermediate' school before entry into the secondary school. In fact, however, the idea of intermediate or middle school has been abandoned in many African countries as the need to produce educated manpower has increased and because this system is seen as a colonial device to delay the African child's education.

Content of primary school education Whatever system is used in whatever environmental or social conditions, the question of what is to be taught is still of extreme importance. Primary education in Africa has been coloured by the fact that the missions, which were the pioneers in education, considered it as a means of carrying on their evangelistic work as well as of spreading literacy. Herein lies the main difference between the policy of the missions and the state on education. For the church, education is a process for nurturing the child to come to the fullness of life – it has both a moral and a spiritual function. For the state, on the other hand, education is a social service which is expected by the general public. Primary education in particular, from this point of view, should be a means by which the child is prepared to live in his society effectively and creatively. These attitudes determine what shall be given priority in the classroom.

Primary education is generally criticized on the grounds that it has not helped the child to see the relation between what he learns in school and what actually exists or takes place in his everyday life. It was concern for this situation which led the Cambridge Conference on Education in Africa to recommend that 'the basis of the curriculum in the middle school should be a carefully integrated scheme of practical and theoretical work so that the academic work rises always from practical and concrete beginnings'.[1] This recommendation was initiated by the East and Central African group – one of the two groups which made an on-the-spot inquiry into the state of education in British Tropical Africa in preparation for the Cambridge Conference. The Addis Ababa scheme has gone much further than this by calling attention to the need to shift emphasis from philosophical and literary achievement to practical work to meet the needs of modern technological societies.

Curriculum reform   In order to make this shift in the emphasis in both primary and secondary education some radical changes in curriculum have to be made. In general, every primary school system must include the following in what it offers to the child:

(i) Basic tool subjects – reading, writing and arithmetic.

(ii) Knowledge of society and life – history, geography, civics, health, nature study.

(iii) Practical subjects such as handicrafts and gardening.

(iv) Aesthetic and artistic subjects – physical education, drawing, painting, etc.

(v) Religious and moral subjects.

(vi) Language and culture.

Curriculum reform, if it is to be effective, has also to be seen in relation to other aspects of education. First, the materials and their sources must be considered and must make sense within the range of the child's experience. Secondly, consideration must be given to reforms in organization and in methods of teaching. This affects the whole system of teacher-training, as the teacher must be enabled to acquire modern methods of teaching and have access to and make effective use of materials. The school must therefore be well equipped. There is a great need for the recasting of existing textbooks and preferably for the writing of new ones which will take into account the African's background. One problem, however, is that there are very few authors available to do this. There are three schemes at present in operation trying to solve this problem: (a) There is a UNESCO-sponsored scheme of textbook production co-ordinating efforts and giving encouragement to those who are making experiments. The centre of this project is at Yaounde in the Cameroons. (b) There are two Christian Literature Clearing Centres, one at Yaounde, and the other at Mandolo in Zambia. (c) There is an Africa Literature Centre, also in Zambia, which is engaged in the training of Africans in many aspects of literature production.

Curriculum reform is most urgent and necessary in the following subjects:

Subject	Suggested reform
Science	Less learning of theories which are not readily applicable to the child's experience. Science to help in the problems of life. Reform in methods of science teaching, placing emphasis on observation and experimentation.
Languages	Less emphasis on grammar and syntax, but development of correct use of words and expression both in speech and in writing. Mother tongue to be encouraged, but child should have to learn language that carries him beyond limits of his tribe and country.
History	Memorizing of facts and dates to be replaced by interpretation of events in relation to the present.

	History of the child's immediate society to be given due regard, but this should lead to the history of Africa as a continent and extend to world history.
Geography	Geography teaching should be practical and should involve child's activities. Memorizing of meaningless data should be discouraged. The human approach should replace emphasis on regional studies.

We can see from the above that more than revision of the syllabus is required and that many factors are involved. Curriculum reform is often necessitated by a crisis in education, or general discontent of the public, especially parents and employers, but political and social pressures also play a significant part. Actual reform, or for that matter revision, is usually a task for specialists, education officers, teachers or professors, and psychologists; very often parents are brought in also. The teacher should plan an ever-increasing role in curriculum reform or in syllabus revision because of his intimate knowledge of the ability of the child who has to use it.

The secondary level of education

The foregoing discussion has already implied the problems of the secondary level of education to which curriculum reform applies even more seriously, because of the prominent place which the new nations are giving to secondary education in their plans for educational development and expansion.

Secondary education is defined by the Addis Ababa Conference as the level of education which 'with the variations required by particular circumstances, may consist of a further six years of school life in two stages'.[2] The two stages envisaged are the lower and the higher stages of secondary education, about 12-15 and 16-18 years respectively, with slight variations.

It is important to emphasize that secondary education as defined above includes all forms of further education beyond the primary level. It includes vocational schools, technical institutions and teacher-training at a pre-university level, as well as more academically biassed schools, often called 'grammar schools'. From this, it will be seen that the function of secondary education is twofold. On the one hand, it is expected to prepare young people for entry into the professions; on the other hand, it must prepare those few who are to go on to

university and similar institutions. In this respect the expansion of
university education is dependent on the quality of the secondary
school. The Addis Ababa plan envisages a system of education where
30% of those completing primary schooling should be able to go on
to secondary school. Of this 30%, 20% should go on to vocational
and technical education and teacher-training and 10% to general
academic schooling, of whom perhaps one half may proceed to
university.

The length of secondary education in general is six years, but
there are slight variations according to the degree of development in
different countries. In many countries, secondary school is not started
until twelve or thirteen. In these countries the secondary school
course is generally divided into two stages, as outlined above.

The Addis Ababa plan gives three reasons why the development
of secondary education should be the first priority : first, this important stage has suffered neglect in the past; secondly, economic
development depends upon the phenomenal expansion of secondary
education facilities in order to raise the necessary skilled manpower
resources; thirdly, development of university education which the
new nations enthusiastically desire will depend on sufficient numbers coming out of the secondary schools to enter universities when
these are established.

African states have been enjoined to pay particular attention to the
development of secondary education, and the Addis Ababa Conference hoped that through support from international resources
together with local efforts, secondary school enrolment would be
raised from 903,700 in 1961 to nearly two millions in 1966 and about
six millions in 1981. The effect of this call is already beginning to
be felt and some measure of success has been achieved. While the
plan still remains an ideal for some countries, others have exceeded
the targets. The ·Cambridge Conference drew attention to this problem and the Addis Ababa Conference made the African states resolve
to do something about it. That the new nations mean business in
making such a decision is quite clear. Already in November 1963 the
Minister of Education in Malawi announced that 'expansion of
secondary school facilities had priority in the Government's educational programme'. Another announcement came from Tanzania.
The International Development Association had given over 4½ mil-

lion dollars development credit to Tanzania in order to help the government to finance the expansion of its secondary school system. In the Zambia Development Plan, expenditure on education included nearly two and a half million pounds out of a total allocation to education of nearly four and a half million pounds.[3] This is the pattern that has continued in the development of African education since 1961.

Technical education and vocational training

For a long time technical education was conceived only as a means of providing skills and for training useful craftsmen. The term usually used was 'industrial education' and this aimed at introducing the African pupil to the life of industrial society. Training consisted of simple instructions in useful crafts such as building, carpentry, shoemaking and tailoring, all of which were of immediate appeal and an answer to the people's needs. Technical education as an alternative to post-primary education is a relatively new idea in Africa. The second stage in the development of technical education was the establishment of trades schools in which instructions in the theory and practice of trades and crafts were given. In many countries these trades schools still continue to be the main source of craftsmen and artisans. Trades schools have suffered from the idea that everyone with a given skill can become an 'instructor'. This has resulted in a generally low standard at these schools, and industry and commerce have been hesitant to absorb trainees from them. This has created frustration and unemployment. In some countries plans have been made to introduce technical education at a level at which it can provide an alternative to other professional training.

Post-secondary technical education

Pressed by the needs of development plans and expanding economies, African states have turned their attention to the urgent need for skilled men and women in large numbers. As a consequence, technical education has received more attention in the past few years than it has ever had before. This has led to the establishment of a large number of technical schools and colleges. Five years after the Second World War, the Government of Nigeria, for example, had been able to establish a number of important centres of technical education. Of these centres, Zaria has held the leading position in the training of young Nigerians in arts and science. Technical schools giving education parallel to that given in the secondary schools are gradually replacing the old trades schools. In Tanzania, trades schools have been upgraded. In Zambia, one trades school has been raised to the status of a technical college preparing students both for the local qualifying examinations and the external examinations of the London City and Guilds. These examples are indicative of the general trend.

In French-speaking Africa, technical education had for long been given great importance in the education systems, but the general attitude did not differ much from that which prevailed in the English speaking countries. In the Cameroons, as in most French-speaking countries and in the Congos, there are still numerous centres in which instruction in such important fields of technology as engineering, electrical installation and motor mechanics is given. In these countries, as in English-speaking Africa, phenomenal development has taken place in the field of technical education mainly through upgrading and refitting existing crafts schools, by establishing new, modern centres, and by employing better trained instructors.

There are also schools which offer practical professional training for junior ranks in commerce and government administration, for example, junior clerks, typists, community development assistants and social welfare workers. The importance of such institutions lies in their creating well-informed and reasonably trained citizens, whether or not they engage in these professions. These schools are now attracting fairly large numbers of girls in some countries, which is an important development for Africa.

Higher technical education

As technical education is now considered to be the key to economic development, every country in Africa is giving attention and resources to the building of better technical schools and is encouraging universities to establish faculties or departments of science and technology. A number of universities now have such faculties. In Nigeria there are faculties of science and technology at University College, Ibadan, the University of Nigeria, Nsuka, and the University of Ife. In Ghana such facilities exist at the University of Science and Technology, Kumasi; in East Africa at the University College, Nairobi; in the Congo at the Lovanium University in Kinshasa and at the State University of Lubumbashi. Ethiopia, Liberia, Madagascar, Sierra Leone, the Sudan and Zambia all have universities with faculties or departments of science and technology.

Agricultural education

The importance of agricultural education in Africa must be seen in relation to the needs and geographical distribution of the population. The bulk of the population lives in rural areas and these people depend for their livelihood on natural resources, particularly agriculture. Plans for economic development have therefore to take serious account of the needs of rural communities. Agricultural development is going to be the testing ground of the viability of national development plans and a proof of the desire for diversification of the national economies. Consequently, agricultural education will need to be given more attention than it has had in the past.

The dissemination of knowledge of modern methods of cultivation and crop management and the raising of standards of agricultural production have been made difficult by the general attitude of Africans to manual labour. The attraction of academic education has been such that a great many educated young men and women shun any work in which they have to use their hands, especially work on the land. This, in turn, has caused able-bodied men and women to move to the urban areas in search of work and fortune. This search often ends in frustration, as there are simply not enough of the right kind of white-collar jobs to go round.

To remedy this situation the importance and dignity of labour and the honour of working with one's own hands needs to be emphasized at an early stage of education. The other problem to be faced is the resistance of the rural communities to any change in agricultural methods. If production is to be increased without impoverishing the soil such changes are essential and it is therefore important that education should enlighten present attitudes. Rural communities must be led to see the superiority of the new methods, rather than coerced into using them by government measures. In this way soil erosion, caused by overgrazing, deforestation and careless cultivation, and soil exhaustion caused by lack of crop-rotation may be checked.

These problems necessitate a change in the policy of agricultural education. The idea of 'gardening' as a subject in the curriculum of primary and secondary schools must give place to the teaching of general science with emphasis on the study of plant and animal life, while facilities must be provided for agricultural education at a higher level. This policy is reflected in the establishment of agricultural colleges in all parts of Africa and there is now in general a scientific approach to agricultural education.

Teacher-training

There are the following levels of teacher-training in Africa: (a) a two or three year post-primary course in which one year is spent learning English and other school subjects in order to give the students some academic background for professional training; (b) a post-secondary course which is gaining ground and may soon become the minimum form of teacher-training in most countries; (c) a post-school certificate course for teachers in the higher stage of primary schools; (d) teacher-training as a form of higher education. The Addis Ababa Plan envisages a teacher population of one million for Africa South of the Sahara by 1980; and it emphasizes the need for properly trained staff and for the elimination of the untrained teacher. All types of teacher-training schools are going to be urged to increase their facilities but this must be done without lowering professional standards. In many countries, the 'Vernacular Teacher Training' schools are being discontinued because the inadequate background of the entrants means that they do not profit from training in modern methods. Better-trained teachers must be produced in large numbers if education systems are to be efficient, and countries to increase their trained manpower resources. Teacher-training parallel with secondary education will continue to be the main means of supply of teachers for elementary schools but facilities for teacher-training at an advanced level must be seen as an important investment for the future. A number of universities have programmes of post-graduate teacher-training and those which have not already established these should be encouraged to do so as soon as conditions and finances make it possible. Government co-operation should be sought in all cases.

Higher education and university expansion

The UNESCO Conference on the Development of Higher Education in Africa gave a working definition of this level of education as 'all types of education of an institutional nature (academic, professional, technological, teacher education) such as universities, university colleges, liberal art colleges, technological institutes, and teacher-training colleges, for which the basic entrance requirement is completion of a full secondary education, of which the usual entrance age is about 18 years, and in which the courses lead to the giving of a named award (degree, diploma or certificate of higher studies)'.[4]

This is a very useful definition because it takes a wide view of higher education and is in itself descriptive of the processes of education beyond the secondary level. It is an advance over the once prevailing definition of higher education in Africa as simply university education, which resulted in confusion when it was attempted to establish comparable standards in the French and English systems. The new definition makes this task much easier and goes a long way towards unifying the educational systems in Africa.

For the purpose of this study we shall use two terms: the 'university' and 'other forms of higher education'. The Tananarive Conference considered the establishment and development of higher education institutions as basic to the social and economic development of the African nations, particularly because of the need for high level manpower resources. The conference further faced some fundamental questions regarding the role of the university in African society and rightly pointed out that African universities will need to take account of changing conditions and demands without using these as an excuse for isolation and the lowering of academic standards. International links and internationally accepted standards must be maintained while catering for internal needs.

University expansion

University development in Africa has been lamentably slow. There are several reasons for this, but the main ones are lack of money and the small number of secondary school leavers. University education has been a luxury for the privileged few with money and time.

It is unlikely that there will be any dramatic change in this situation, for university education, though not necessarily a luxury, could never become universal because of its nature and the purpose it tries to fulfil. Universities must, of necessity, be highly selective.

The university must fulfil its role not only as an institution of higher education but also as the centre of the community and the custodian of the best that society has achieved in its development. In the African situation the university should also be a source of inspiration in the battle against ignorance, disease and poverty.

Consolation can be found in future prospects but the present position, taken alone, is desperate. In the 1961-2 period there were only 41,000 students enrolled in all forms of higher education, and this includes those studying outside Africa. During this period there were only thirty-one institutions of university status but in most countries there were also other institutions of higher learning such as technical colleges and professional colleges.

The year 1961-2 was, in fact, one of phenomenal development of universities and similar institutions in most of the independent countries probably because of the number of countries which gained independence during this period. Nevertheless, by 1966-7 the number of students and full-time staff was still small, as is shown by Table IV.

TABLE IV: University Enrolment and Number of Full-time Teaching and Administrative Staff 1966-7

		Enrolment 1966-7	Full-time academic staff
Angola	Estudios Gervais Universitarios (1962)	53	12
Burundi	Universitiye Officalle de Bujumbura (1961)	222	28
C. A. Republic	Member of Group of Institutions for Higher Education (1961)		
Cameroon	Université fédérale du Cameroun (1962)	210	40
Congo Brazza	Member of Group of Institutions of Higher Education		

		Enrolment 1966-7	Full-time academic staff
Congo Kinshasa	1. Université Lovanium (1949)	2038	202
	2. Université Officialle de Congo (1960)	500	100
	3. Université Libre du Congo in Kisangani several professional schools		
Dahomey & Togo	Sub-University Courses		
Ethiopia	1. Haile Selassie I University (1961)	2828	365
	2. University of Asmera (1964)	1222	41 (81)
Gabon	Member of Groups of Institutions for Higher Education		
Guinea	A number of professional institutions (1963)	130	70
Ivory Coast	Université d'Abidjan (1963)	1676	99
Liberia	University of Liberia (1951)	890	124
Malagasy Republic	Université de Madagascar (1961)	3107	146
Mali	Sub-University Courses		
Mozambique	Estudios Gervais Universitarios du Mozambique (1962)	392	109
Rwanda	Université Nationale du Rwanda (1963)	130	27
Senegal	Université de Dakar (1957)	3143	240
Somalia	Instito Universitarios del Somalia (1959)	–	–
Sudan	1. University of Khartoum (1956)	3060	–
	2. University of Cairo Khartoum Branch (1959)	1800	?
Togo	Institut d'Enseignement Supérieur de Benin (1965)	117	10

COMMONWEALTH

		Enrolment 1966-7	Full-time academic staff
Ghana	1. University of Ghana (1961)	2445	392
	2. University College of G. Coast (1962)	1055	125
	3. University of Science and Technology (1961)	1549	203
Nigeria	1. University of Ife (1961)	1647	267
	2. University of Lagos (1962)	1764	232
	3. University of Nigeria (*reopened in March 1970 after civil war*)	2587	360
East Africa	1. University College Nairobi (1961)	1748	322
	2. University College Dar-es-Salaam (1961)	1227	230
	3. Makerere University College (1922)	2219	242
Lesotho	University of Botswana, Lesotho and Swaziland (1964)	383	61
Malawi	University of Malawi	819	124
Sierra Leone	1. Fourah Bay College (1827 and 1926)	604	96
	2. Njala University College (1964)	297	93
Rhodesia	University College of Rhodesia and Nyasaland (1953)	857	195
Zambia	University of Zambia	991	211

Some of these institutions developed out of existing technical and teacher-training colleges. This period of expansion had come to an end by 1964 largely because of lack of staff and financial resources. Very limited advance in university expansion has been made since then and, as can be seen, in 1966-7 there were only just over 36,000 students studying in universities in Africa itself. Moreover, all the existing university institutions are at present staffed preponderantly by expatriate personnel. The number of nationals on the staff of university institutions at present varies from country to country, but is rarely more than 20%.[5] The Addis Ababa Plan aims to reverse this ratio by 1980. The Tananarive Conference on the Development of Higher Education in Africa suggests that the remedy for this problem would be to accept the fact that African nationals have had less opportunity for preparation for university teaching and that requirements for appointment should therefore be less exacting. For example, assistant lecturers with first university degrees could be taken on and provided with opportunities for studying for appropriate higher qualifications. Also, salary scales need to be adjusted so that they are in relation to those of the senior civil service. At the same time attractive terms including incentives have to be considered in order to attract expatriate staff. This should not, however, lead to discrimination in the matter of basic salary scales between nationals and expatriates.

It is debatable what should be the content of education at this level. Higher education has to pay due regard to the matter of imparting knowledge, but it also has a duty to society as a whole and has to play its part in all forms of national development by producing high-level personnel. The curricula should therefore endeavour to integrate the university with the economic and social life of the nation. The Tananarive Conference has drawn attention to the importance of teaching African studies. These should include the study of African cultures, language and literature, customs, and social and political institutions. In this and other ways the universities in Africa could develop their own particular character but, for success, the syllabuses of the first degree courses would have to be broadened.[6]

Most of the universities in Africa have departments of extra-mural studies. The University of Ghana has an Institute of Public Education; Ibadan has a well-run Department of Extra-Mural Studies; Makerere University has its extra-mural work spread in the three East African territories of Uganda, Kenya and Tanzania. The University College of Sierra Leone, Fourah Bay College, has a Department of Extra-Mural Studies and the University of Zambia has a Department of Extra-Mural Studies and also runs correspondence courses. This is an important step and present results show beyond doubt that it is possible to provide university education by such means.

These departments are of great importance in any country because they enable men and women to receive higher education who would never otherwise have had the chance to do so. In this way also political and social responsibility can be aroused. In Africa increasing importance is being placed on the study of society and the role of African nations in the world community, but normal university subjects can also be studied in courses leading to degrees and diplomas.

NOTES

1. Cambridge Report on African Education, p. 93.
2. UNESCO/ECA. Final Report: Conference of African States on the Development of Education in Africa, 1961, p. 48.
3. African Education: Annual Summary for the year 1962, Government Printed, Lusaka 1963.
4. The Development of Higher Education in Africa, Preface, UNESCO, 1962.
5. Information taken from the *International Handbook of Universities and other Institutions of Higher Education 1968*; The International Association of Universities, Paris 1968; and the *Commonwealth Universities Year Book 1970*, The Association of Commonwealth Universities, London 1970.
6. H.M. Committee for Higher Education Report, HMSO, paras. 262, 263.

6

Adult Education

Adult education was given as the third priority in the plans for educational expansion which were established by the Conference of African States on the Development of Education in Africa. Adult education is urgently needed to cut down the high rate of illiteracy and to counteract the appalling drop-out rate from primary and secondary schools. Also, many primary and secondary school children have to return to illiterate communities where what they have gained from their few years of education is often very soon forgotten. The existence of a large illiterate and ignorant community is not only a serious challenge but also a national liability, as it is a handicap on economic development. Adult education is very important, therefore, if literacy is to be increased and ignorance reduced, and if the deficiencies caused by incomplete schooling are to be overcome.

Definitions of the term adult education vary and there has been some confusion in the past because of differences in the interpretation of its aims and functions. For some, adult education may simply mean instruction and activities of an educational value given to adults, while for others it may include a complex system of post-school education. The latter is perhaps the most useful definition of adult education because it takes a broad view of its functions and goals. This is what we shall have in mind in this context when we consider adult education – the all-inclusive pattern of adult development which has in view the need of the adult not only as an individual but also as a member of his community and which helps him to live more effectively in his society. On the basis of this definition, adult education will include mass education and community development, vocational training, learning of reading, writing and arithmetic, youth activities and formal and informal education aimed at training the adult for his duties as a citizen of his state. As in the education of children, educators of adults must try to discover how best to present knowledge in the context of the adults' own social, cultural and economic conditions. In this way the adult will be enabled to relate the knowledge he has attained to the life that he lives in the community and to make such education relevant, useful and significant.

In Western countries where adult education has had a long history, its development has been conceived as a process directed towards the creating of a literate and well-informed public. For this reason the question of giving men and women new skills to do new jobs is not of crucial importance. In Africa, however, adult education will need to be designed to meet both these needs. It is as important to raise living standards and to equip men and women for the development programmes as it is to help them to develop their personalities. Adult education has an important role in relation to community development especially in providing training in simple skills. A variety of skills are taught in addition to general instruction in reading, writing and arithmetic, such skills as basketry, pottery, woodcarving, sewing and needlework. To these should also be added civic education, which is taught when the adult has reached the stage at which he can read well. This subject should include local history and general information on forms of local and central government.

Many of the African countries are finding that their efforts to promote new schemes of adult education are handicapped by lack of personnel with specialized skills in their field and also by lack of sufficient material for further work once the students are able to read and work on their own. There is nothing more discouraging for the teachers than to make people literate and then to have nothing for them to read. The problem arises from the multiplicity of local languages and dialects which makes the work of production and publication of books and other materials not only very difficult but also expensive. Much thinking and co-operative action is needed if a solution is to be found to this problem. The answer would seem to lie in the reduction of languages and dialects in any one given area to a manageable number, but this is an onerous task as each tribe, however small, wants its language to be preserved. Another solution is the adoption of English or French in schools, but this is difficult because of the need to help people develop their culture and local history and language. The problem needs to be looked at from an all-Africa angle, and this is one very important area in which the new states in Africa can co-operate by co-ordinating their efforts and resources and by soliciting international assistance. For this reason UNESCO's attempts to establish literature centres should be welcomed and encouragement and support given by the governments concerned to voluntary agencies engaged in literature production. First in this group are the churches and missions who are not only pioneers in literature production for Africa, but are also engaged in training writers and editors. This contribution by the churches to education is a very important one.

All major conferences on education have tried to grapple with the problem of lack of material but have always come up against difficulties. The Conference on Adult Education which was held in Montreal in Canada in 1960 took up this matter seriously and recommended that governments and other agencies must be more concerned if progress was to be made in this field. The Conference of African States on the Development of Education in 1961 at Addis Ababa proposed that attention be given to the production of literature and textbooks, and now steps are being taken to this end.

The new understanding of the place of adult education should lead to governments and educators taking greater interest in the field and in this way to more financial support than has been given in the past. There are encouraging signs of co-operation in the field of adult education between governments, local authorities and other voluntary bodies such as churches and industrial concerns. One of the problems to be overcome in the next few years is that of finding and retaining trained personnel in large enough numbers, and of organizing and mobilizing voluntary assistance.

This general survey of adult education should provide sufficient background for the rather more detailed discussion which follows in the rest of this chapter. Among other things we shall discuss the significance of adult education in national development. We shall also consider the question of responsibility for the development of adult education.

Forms of adult education in Africa

The discussion that follows will attempt to give an evaluation of the effectiveness of the different forms of adult education. It will also indicate the areas in which there is need for new development.

Types of adult education current in many African countries range from mass literacy programmes to university extra-mural courses and correspondence courses. About ten or fifteen years ago much attention was focused on mass literacy and fundamental education, as it was believed that this was the key to development and to overcoming the problems that beset Africa. To try and meet the challenge presented by the illiteracy rate experiments were made with methods of teaching African adults to read and write in the shortest possible time. One example is the method in which the laborious learning of the alphabet is reduced to a minimum by integrating the learning process through sight and sound, that is by a combination of words and pictures on the basis of syllable units. In this system the material presented is graduated so as to enable the learner to go progressively from simple to complex constructions. One advantage of this method is that the learner's interest is aroused by the fact that, right from the beginning, he is reading significant words and phrases and later on sentences.

An example of a mass literacy campaign on this basis, which the author observed, is that carried out in the Copperbelt area of Zambia. There a modified Laubach system of teaching reading and writing was employed with remarkable success. In the years immediately after the Second World War, voluntary agencies supported by government grants directed their attention to a mass literacy operation. Teams of instructors were trained for the purpose of supervising the operations but the main technique was to use the new literates to teach others as much as they themselves had learned. The popular description of this method is 'each-one-teach-one'. Reading and writing groups were a common feature in the quarters where miners lived. Similar scenes were also common in villages where the teams had operated. After a few years, however, the initial interest wore off and the phenomenal increase in literacy which had been forecast did not materialize. There were three main reasons for this lack of lasting success: (a) The deficiencies inherent in the method itself which tends to give many people a veneer of literacy from which they soon lapse; (*b*) lack of reading matter for the new literates. There should be graded, well-produced and tested reading matter before schemes of mass literacy are started; (*c*) lack of worthwhile motivation in the people who were being trained to read – evidence of interest and the will to learn has been observed where mass literacy programmes have been directly related to some economic pursuit. Economic communities provide a concentrated field and the results are rewarding and lasting.

In the case of the Copperbelt Campaign a small press was set up at Mindolo, Kitwe, to produce primers and reading matter, but the materials had been hurriedly produced so that the quality was poor. Perhaps a lack of success was to be expected where the reason for starting a scheme was that officials felt there ought to be a need for it rather than because there was an actual public demand for it.

A second type of adult education is what we may call 'follow-up' education. It is adult education given in a more classroom fashion than the mass literacy education. It could be a direct follow-up of the literacy operation to introduce the newly initiated literate to the use of his newly acquired ability and to start him on an educational course where regular attendance begins to be the determining factor in the progress which the learner makes. At present the curriculum follows closely that of either the primary or secondary schools. The earlier stages are fortunately not yet dominated by examinations, but at the higher stages of the primary curriculum, teachers and learners begin to be preoccupied with preparation for examinations and certificates.

In this connection the night-school is of particular importance in African adult education. The desire to gain knowledge for its own sake is a very strong incentive for adult education. At present the night-schools are more a feature of the urban areas, but in some rural areas late afternoon classes are held in the classrooms of the village school. However, the village school timetable often limits the time available for adult education. Two sessions a day are quite common, and teachers are often so tired by the end of a school day that they are unable to take on more teaching responsibility after their normal work. In this respect, rural adult education is at a great disadvantage because there are few people who can be used as substitutes for school teachers. In urban centres, on the other hand, it is possible to mobilize young professionals such as clerks, hospital orderlies, social welfare workers, shopkeepers and others for this purpose.

At the secondary stage of adult education correspondence courses have become important. In Africa, where educational facilities have lagged far behind the demands for secondary education, the correspondence college has assumed far greater significance than in some other parts of the world. These are 'knowledge-canning' centres where shelves are laden with piles of carefully prepared lectures. Fortunately it is an expensive business to establish correspondence colleges and Africa does not seem to be in danger of being flooded with quack colleges. It costs as much as £2,000 to prepare lectures in a subject at GCE 'O' level, in addition to which there would be expenses for the payment of tutors to mark papers and revise lectures.

Correspondence courses have proved a boon for the African adult who wants to improve himself. Not all who enrol in the correspondence courses succeed and there is, in fact, a high drop-out rate, but for those who stick it, and are able to discipline themselves in the use of their leisure, there are handsome rewards.

Adult education at the university level

Some of the correspondence schools, particularly those operating from Britain and South Africa, have courses ranging from the lowest stage of secondary education to university degrees. Adult education at university level is particularly important for two reasons. Firstly, at the university level the need for personal contact both with the tutors and the other students increases, and the necessity for testing knowledge by personal engagement in dialogue and debate becomes imperative. There are too few universities in Africa to make this type of education possible for all. This makes it the more necessary that all university establishments should use their resources and facilities to the maximum so as to help as many people as possible. Secondly, the establishment of a university in many an African country is widening the gap in that country between the masses and the small *élite*. For both these reasons the university extra-mural department should be seen as a necessary part of university development and expansion. Happily, most of the existing universities have created extra-mural sections, in one form or another, although in some instances this part of the university programme is a mere appendix to the university organization and often the requirements for the staff are much less exacting than for their colleagues in the faculties. There are often only one or two people in this section of the university, working under difficult conditions. The situation is somewhat different in universities where the adult education programme is organized either as an institute or as a department. Good examples are the University of Rhodesia which has an Institute of Adult Education, and the University of Ghana which has replaced what was the Department of Extra-Mural Study by an Institute of Public Education. The University of Zambia has both a programme of extra-mural studies and a well-organized department for correspondence courses. This is a hopeful trend towards providing for the specific educational needs of adults whose education has left many gaps. University programmes of adult education are very much helped where there is an active voluntary adult education organization such as the People's Educational Association of Ghana. Such voluntary organizations are not only important in terms of co-ordination and organization, but also in providing a body which watches and endeavours to protect adult education interests. Such a body has the advantage of being free from political or partisan pressures.

Development of residential adult colleges

Of particular interest in the development of adult education at a higher level is the residential college. Residential colleges are centres which are usually autonomous and designed for citizenship education. There are at present very few such institutions in Africa, but the success of some of these colleges should encourage the establishment of more. In the establishment of residential adult centres, voluntarism is an important ingredient, but government support should be sought where voluntary contribution cannot sustain the establishment. The emphases differ from one college to another in view of the need to relate such institutions to the needs of the local community and the nature of the national development. Three examples

are the Kikuyu College of Social Science near Nairobi in Kenya, the
Kivukoni College in Dar-es-Salaam in Tanzania, the College of
Citizenship in Salisbury, Rhodesia, and the more advanced College
for Further Education in Lusaka, Zambia. In Zambia there is also
in the process of development the President's College of Citizenship,
which in character and programme will be similar to Kikuyu College
and Kivukoni College in Kenya and Tanzania respectively.

There are other similar institutions going by names such as study
and research centres. In these colleges the emphasis is on educating
for leadership, with a curriculum flexible enough to meet immediate
and urgent needs. In these centres there are three main subjects:
Social Studies, Citizenship and Civic Subjects, and Economics.

The students at these institutions are men and women between
the ages of twenty-five and fifty, who come for short or long periods
of residential training. The Kikuyu College is essentially a vocational
college, but the curriculum allows for much freedom in debate, lectures, seminars and the discussion of topics of vital interest for the
student in his contribution to economic development.

It should also be pointed out that much of the work of the new
conference and ecumenical centres is aimed at adult leadership education. The Limuru Conference Centre near Nairobi is one such centre.
A similar institution is the Mindolo Ecumenical Foundation near
Kitwe in Zambia, which has residential courses in journalism and
literature production, national development, community development,
Christian leadership and home economics. Similar centres are now
being planned for Nigeria, Ghana, Tanzania, the Cameroons and
Madagascar through the machinery of the Inter-Church Aid Service
of the World Council of Churches. The Inter-Church Aid Service
is directed by the World Council of Churches, which receives re-
quests from churches through a project list, and serves as a clearing
house for the funds that are received from the donor churches. All
these projects for conference and study centres are hoping to get
initial assistance from this source.

Content and curriculum

The curriculum for an adult education programme should be planned
in relation to the current needs of the community in which the adult
lives and in relation to the adult's own needs. At the mass education

level the matter is quite simple, as the learner is primarily interested in being able to read and write on his own. His greatest ambition is to be able to write his own letters to relatives and to read books such as, for Christians (and even many non-Christians), the bible. At this level the important thing is not so much what is taught as how it is taught. Reading and writing should be taught effectively and in the shortest possible time. Even in the matter of methodology there is choice only between the repetition method and the more proven method of sight and sound. The important thing here is that the material should be carefully graded and should make sense in the context of the social and cultural life of the learner. It therefore follows that the material must be presented in the learner's own language.

Adult education as a follow-up education is by no means so simple. There is the question, for example, of whether or not this type of education should be identical with either the normal primary or secondary education. The adults themselves see their education in terms of a short-cut to normal primary education which leads to a tendency to study for examinations and certificates.

The dilemma, therefore, is that educators have no convincing reasons why the adult should not attain his objectives by following the curriculum of the primary and secondary school. The way out seems to lie in linking adult education to community life and the manifold activities of the business of daily living. This would essentially differentiate adult education from child education, even if the same subjects were taught; the essential difference being that for the child the necessity for applied knowledge of his subjects can be deferred to a later stage, while for the adult, whatever stage of education he has reached, it is very important that what he is learning should be applied to life. Secondly, the adult, in contrast to the child, is greatly assisted by his experience of life even though he may, from the point of school education, be backward. Important ideas can more easily be understood and interpreted. For this reason adult education curricula could be diversified to include social and political education as well as school education. In terms of the curriculum, therefore, adult education beyond the literacy stage could be constructed so as to include the following nine groups of subjects:

1. Tool subjects: Reading, writing and arithmetic.

2. Languages: the mother tongue should have priority but trans-tribal and international languages should also be studied.

3. The study of human society: this should include history, geography, social and civic studies.

4. Sciences, both general and applied.

5. Health education: this should include hygiene and sanitation.

6. Cultural and aesthetic education, including drama, music, folk-lore, drawing, painting, sculpture and engraving.

7. Home economics: these subjects should be related to the needs of the community and the learner.

8. Practical subjects such as African handicrafts using local material, hobbies and simple modern techniques.

9. Physical education, including games.

This list is just an outline, and detailed construction of the syllabus is a very specialized business. It is not intended to give the idea that adult education in Africa is well organized and planned, but simply to indicate the areas which adult education in Africa should endeavour to cover. The syllabus for each subject is a matter for the educators and educational administrators. At the level of extra-mural or university extension courses the matter of curriculum planning becomes a complex affair because of the high degree of specialization involved, but the basic needs of the adult and his community must always be taken into account even at this level.

Responsibility and resources

Responsibility for the operation of adult education has often been decided on the basis of immediate local needs and there is no one pattern in all African countries. Thus, for example, for reasons of expediency a mining company or a factory management may become indirectly involved in the programme of adult education. Not only is this to the benefit of the workers but also is in the interest of the management because a measure of education, however limited, cultivates understanding, and understanding can lead to increased productivity. This involvement ranges from the systematic release of employees for adult education classes, to the running of efficient systems of adult education such as, for example, the educational and training schemes of the copper mines in Zambia. In such cases the full responsibility and financial provision rests with the agency involved. However, the government concerned usually takes an interest in these operations and may offer technical advice. In the case cited here the mining company's education division has co-operated with the Ministry of Education.

Education of the adult aimed at community and social betterment is more often the responsibility of the community development or social welfare departments of central and local government than of the Ministry of Education. In many countries there is a Ministry of Social Welfare and Community Development. In Zambia, for instance, a number of area training centres have been established in which the main emphasis is on the teaching of simple skills and crafts to villagers, but which also includes programmes of mass literacy. In the urban areas the municipal authorities have established community centres where, among other things, adult education classes are also conducted. Such centres, however, seldom make an assessment of the task undertaken because of the pressure of needs and the inability of the statutory system to provide them. Community development programmes and informal education are the prerogative of the urban housing departments of municipal councils.

Formal or follow-up education in the form of extension classes and evening classes is usually under the direct responsibility of the education department. However, there are many countries in Africa in which, either in addition to this or because of the absence of it, voluntary agencies organize programmes of adult education. The case of the copper mines of Zambia which run adult education programmes for their employees has already been cited, but special mention must also be made of the work of the missions and churches in Africa which are important and very successful agencies for adult education. In their mission centres or compounds and their scattered outposts, churches carry out a diversified education programme including mass education and more advanced classes of adult education. Governments have generally recognized the importance of this contribution so that in many countries such work receives government grants.

At the extra-mural level, adult education becomes the direct responsibility of the university, which assumes full authority in the matter of the syllabus and in the appointment of teachers. However, the university usually receives grants from the state for this work which is generally regarded as a necessary addition to its 'normal work'. In this way extra-mural courses enjoy general academic freedom under the umbrella of the university although in situations where there are strained relations between the university and the government, the first section of the university programme to suffer is the extra-mural section. This is because the authorities fear that the adult learner who still remains part of the community might be a political risk. His studies might lead to a critical examination of the political and social institutions of his country if they are followed in an atmosphere of unbounded freedom. This may ultimately lead to open criticism and questioning of the policies of his government. Also, in the final analysis, the responsibility for financing these courses and sometimes for their supervision as well lies with the state.

In a few cases, particularly where the church is involved, the whole cost may be borne by the voluntary agency concerned. Even in such cases, however, the time usually comes when the burden becomes too heavy and government support has to be sought.

In recent years adult education in Africa has assumed international importance. Through UNESCO, the United Nations has a department of adult education. Its primary interest is in mass education. UNESCO maintains advisory services which are available to both members and non-members of the United Nations. One of its special services is training teachers for education in literacy, but it also encourages experiments and acts as a clearing house for the exchange of information and experience between member countries. In this respect the services of UNESCO in the field of education have continued to increase and to be effective. All countries are now seriously concerned about the problem of illiteracy because it poses a formidable obstacle to economic and social development. The need for assistance in the field of education is therefore enormous.

Training of personnel

At present the general attitude, both of the public and educationists, is that anyone with a fair amount of education at primary level and above could be employed as a teacher in adult classes. The result is that the standard of instruction in many adult classes is appallingly poor and uninteresting. Moreover, it is almost a general practice to consider adult teaching as intrinsically part-time work. Consequently, very little attention is given to the quality of staff and the numbers of teachers needed. By the same token, little or no public funds are made available for adult education programmes.

At present there are no facilities for specialized training of teachers. The general practice in many countries in Africa is to draw the teaching staff for adult classes from the ranks of primary and secondary school teachers. While these teachers are generally equipped with the training and techniques of teaching, some specialist training of those who choose to make adult education their specialized teaching career is needed. One way of doing this might be to add to the general teacher training course a supplementary course in adult education. In practice this would mean the addition of subjects such as Principles of Adult Education, the Study of Society and Group Relations. The ordinary subject of Method of Teaching might be extended to include the conduct of seminars and discussion groups, while Educational Psychology could be enriched by extending it to cover the adult learning process. Facilities for practical work and demonstration must always be an important consideration. These supplementary courses would probably involve an extra year.

Selection of personnel for adult education is as important as training itself. Teaching adults is quite different from teaching young children. Adults require a great deal of patience and resourcefulness from the teacher. They expect to be treated as individuals and their lack of academic knowledge does not always mean that they lack wisdom and responsibility in their dealing with the problems of life. Capacity for natural leadership is a great asset for adult education personnel. A teacher will be respected by the adult learner not because of his age but because of his ability to help them to understand things which they want to learn. This ability depends on the amount of preparation the teacher puts into his work. Specialized training is one way in which the teacher can gain special skills for the teaching of the adult and consequently is of importance if the courses are to be used to full advantage.

The fact that African nations have agreed to attach special attention to the development of adult education indicates that they will also give attention to the selection, training and employment of specially trained men and women. To attract the best men and women, conditions of employment and salaries for adult education teachers will need to be improved considerably. This ought to be the natural development of the new systems of education in Africa as the emphasis is on the economic value of education. The money thus invested would pay handsome dividends.

7

Manpower Development

A great deal has been said about the objectives of education both past and present. The orientation of education towards manpower development is by no means new. This has been one of the main reasons for providing education everywhere; it is a universal idea, the difference lying only in the emphasis of the system in any particular society. Education enables the individual to take his place in society and to respond effectively to the stimuli of his environment. With a change in this environment there is consequent need to make changes in the education the individual receives. Education systems must, therefore, be flexible.

This merely emphasizes the point that education has, as one of its prime purposes, the production of men and women required to operate the intricate machinery of the nation through its many institutions. The most successful education plan, therefore, will enable leaders to emerge, that is leaders equipped to run the social, political and economic systems of the nation.

Manpower development attempts to deal with supply and demand in personnel and to match human resources to the needs of the nation. It is thus the responsibility of the whole nation, for it is important that all should be committed to the objectives of their country. Lack of interest undermines efficiency, and in this way can affect economic prosperity. Men, therefore, are the basis of national development. In the final analysis, it is not the material resources nor the developments in modern technology that matter, it is men, without whom all the best instruments of science and technology are of little use.

Manpower development is only effective if it takes into account the needs of the nation and determines priorities on the basis of these. In Africa the situation cannot be left to take care of itself as African countries do not have a history of education of the right type. Deliberate planning and direction are essential.

Systems of education in newly independent African states must radically change their objectives. The content of education must be so oriented that it will enable nations to produce men and women to man the rapidly developing institutions and structures in the shortest possible time. To do this without undermining the effectiveness and efficiency of these institutions is an onerous task. To this end, African educators, administrators and political leaders need to co-operate in a committed way in order to create a climate in which the young can develop a sense of devotion and patriotic service to their nation. This is the basis of stability in all fields.

Earlier views on education and training

The relating of educational planning to manpower development has been prominently identified as one of the directions education will need to take in Africa. The tendency has been to make the training of men and women for the benefit of national institutions a specialist field.

The training of young people in Africa has been undertaken for different reasons during different periods of development. We have already discussed the missionary motivation in education during the early nineteenth century. The view then was that the task of evangelizing the African people would be impossible without some kind of education, at least advanced enough to enable them to read the bible. During this period a few talented ones were able to advance beyond mere reading and writing and these provided a nucleus of leaders who were able to assist the missionary as evangelists and catechists, and later, as teachers and dispensary assistants.

Later on in the history of the missionary movement in Africa we find another group of men trained at the various mission stations. The needs of the new missionary settlements led to the establishment of permanent institutions – hospitals, schools, and churches. The construction of these required the services of masons, carpenters, and blacksmiths. The mission system produced a number of men reasonably proficient in one or other of these skills. Their contribution can still be seen in the edifices that still exist at these mission stations, some of which show evidence of high quality architecture and workmanship. The greatest contribution of this system to the new nations, however, was the widespread dispersion of these men who can still be seen operating their respective fields in the new industrial society.

Finally, in the mission system of education those few who showed the aptitude and intelligence were used in the role of training itself. Accordingly, those who had advanced beyond the point of simply reading and writing were drafted into teaching others. This group became important and influential and became identified with progress and enlightenment. The teacher in the early African society held a place of high esteem and responsibility comparable with that of the Chief or Headman of the village.

What the missionaries had laboured to produce, colonial administration made good use of. Colonial administrators did not arrive with ready plans to produce manpower to assist them in the gigantic task of bringing order and government to new societies. The few men that the missionary system had produced began to filter through to government administration. These were mostly teachers who had sufficient education to be trained in a limited number of fields, particularly in clerical jobs but also in some other simple professions. The need for educated manpower in the colonial civil service was only minimal since the higher ranks were easily filled by the colonial governments with personnel from the mother country. Africans were only used as junior clerical officers and in similar positions. As a result, no provision was made in many territories for planned training of Africans for administrative positions and for the professions. The exception was the French territories where a policy of assimilation had made it possible for selected Africans to acquire education and training in France. Consequently higher positions were open to them when they returned to Africa. To some extent the policy in Portuguese countries was similar to that of the French but the territories were much less developed.

There were two important reasons for keeping Africans out of senior positions in colonial administration. First, it was thought that the Africans were inherently not as intelligent as the Europeans and therefore would not be able to understand the complicated system of administration. Secondly, the African was foreign to the system of administration and it was thought that a too direct access to the mysteries and secrets of administration might lead to subversion. This attitude was sometimes expressed by saying that the best African was one who was ignorant and therefore no challenge to the authority of the white man. The African who advanced in the colonial system was the one who was docile and submissive.

The Second World War shattered these systems. Africans had become exposed to many other outside influences. During the war many had seen service in other parts of the world and while in the army life had become educated and even qualified in new professions. They had fought the enemy side by side with white men and had in many cases excelled in courageous acts. For the first time Africans realized that they were as good as the white man. On their return these men challenged their society. Those who brought new skills with them desired to be given opportunity to exercise their new talents. They questioned for the first time the basis on which they had been denied opportunities in their home country. The latent African nationalism was aroused and strengthened.

The views held on the training of Africans were overtaken by events over which neither the colonial nor the missionary systems had control. The response to this challenge was half-hearted and at best resulted in job fragmentation; that is, certain jobs previously done by expatriates were 'sacrificed'. Functions which previously were performed by one man would be divided into two or three and the salary for the job was correspondingly fragmented. However, it soon became clear that the events taking place in Africa were moving in favour of the indigenous peoples and that a more realistic policy was to face the fact that the end of the colonial system was in sight. In West Africa the problem of shortage of educated manpower was not a very serious one, since at the time of independence many local persons had already acquired positions of responsibility both in government administration and academic fields, but in East and Central Africa nations started on the road of independence with serious handicaps in this respect.

Manpower projections and directions

One of the problems of educational planning in Africa is that of accurately forecasting national requirements. The rate of change is so rapid that projections are out of date before they are implemented. Innumerable factors may alter original projections. Among these are the human element, social change and political and economic pressures. This emphasizes the importance of flexibility in planning which must always take account of these factors. There must be some relation between expenditure and economic reality. It is most unwise to produce too many skilled or trained men when the economic system of the country is not capable of absorbing them. Where this has happened the result has been an inevitable devaluation of skilled manpower, which in turn creates frustration and chaos in the social structure. Only rigid manpower projections would assume that the needs of today will be the same in the next two or five years, and that the preferences and prestige attached to certain professions will be as they are today.

In many independent countries where national development plans have been drawn up, a great deal of importance has always been attached to manpower development. In these plans, forecasts of manpower requirements have been made in relation to known needs. These projections, however, change as plans are amended or extended. This would seem to indicate that it is not manpower projections which are important but, rather, manpower conservation and direction. The latter two aspects are of particular importance in new nations where manpower resources are limited. Conservation does not mean that the available resources are used sparingly; rather, because of the limitations, what is available is used fully and effectively, in the right place and at the right time. This can be achieved by careful and planned direction of potential and existing resources. Direction is not regimentation but a judicious guiding of potential resources.

Manpower direction can be achieved through different methods depending on the attitudes and expectations of the people to be directed. In a number of countries an educational assessment method is used. This is done by applying aptitude and performance tests, the results of which are then related to the job preferences of the candidate. These tests are given to school leavers in the secondary schools which at the present time are the main source of educated manpower. Another method of manpower direction is simply the placement of secondary school students during vacation in the hope that they may become sufficiently inspired by the prospects of a given profession to want to return to it after leaving school or after some professional training. Another method is that of in-service training in which young men and women are taken on straight from school and under the close supervision of some experienced senior person. In-service training has become one of the most used methods of manpower development in independent Africa. The reason is obvious; shortage of manpower makes the training of personnel away from work a luxury that few can afford. However, the training of persons by this method has its great disadvantages, such as the fact that a good worker may not necessarily be a good trainer. Training is a specialist affair requiring methods which may not be possible on the job because of the desire of management to see that those training make some contribution to production. There is also a feeling amongst those who are being trained that they are wage earners and therefore independent. They would not be as amenable to a disciplined study of the job as would those who are directly undergoing professional training in some training institution.

In-service training is not an ideal method of manpower development but it is suited to Africa because of the generally difficult manpower situation. Its value lies in its capacity to upgrade existing personnel by helping them to have a better understanding of what they are doing, and also by enabling them to gain promotion in their professional fields.

Sources and levels of manpower

One of the many contradictions of the African situation is the persistent existence of unemployment while some industries are desperately short of labour. The problem of unemployment has reached such proportions in some independent African countries that it threatens political and social stability. The difficulty is that while the greatest need is for skilled manpower, the labour force is predominantly unskilled. It is always possible that projects in the national development plans will generate new opportunities for the employment of the non-skilled manpower, but this will always depend on the existence of a nucleus of skilled manpower to direct operations.

These facts emphasize the need for developing manpower resources at as many levels as a nation can afford. At this point it may be interesting to survey the known sources of manpower which for the purpose of this survey can be divided into two broad categories; semi-skilled manpower and educated manpower. Each of these divisions has a number of levels; the former, for instance, would include all kinds of artisans, tradesmen, lower-level technicians and workers who have mastered their trades by physical experience without planned training in theory and practice and without some form of academic qualification or qualifying test or examination. The skilled manpower category would cover a large section of the working population of any developed state and includes skilled and trained technicians, technologists and professionals in all fields and administrators.

Sources of semi-skilled manpower

With the development of secondary industries following on independence, opportunities have been created for those who have aptitude or some kind of education to gain new skills. In this way many unskilled workers have become trained and are able to work with machines. Industry and commerce are the main sources of manpower at this level. As this is such an important aspect of manpower in the sense that these workers constitute the bulk of the working population in the modern cities of new Africa, guidance and even direction at the national level should be considered. The standards of workmanship and quality of national production are to a great extent determined by the amount of government control. In practice this means that the government concerned establishes some machinery for supervision of national and private industries to insure that attention is being paid to the training of workers. Introduction of trade testing would encourage efficiency and would introduce standardization of workmanship. The importance of this section of the working population in the modern African city does not only lie in the fact that they supply semi-skilled workers for the government and industry, but that some of the more successful of the group become the 'self-employed' men who are to be found in large numbers carrying on manufacture of simple products or rendering simple but necessary services to the town population. On their own level in these areas, they create a prosperous and progressive group who make a significant contribution to the economy of the country in general and to industrial development in particular. This group in turn generates opportunity for manpower development because they provide employment for others who are thus enabled to learn new skills. The control of production standards in this section of industry is very difficult, if not impossible, since by and large these concerns operate on an individual basis and are neither recognized nor registered under the normal company law of the land. One way of controlling standards of production among this group would be to encourage and assist them in establishing co-operatives. In this way they would come under the general supervision of the government.

African nations attach great importance to the co-operative movement because of its educational value and because it alleviates labour problems. The co-operative movement holds out great hopes for the improvement of the economic basis of the African nations as through co-operative groups it is possible to conserve limited national resources. There have been failures and disappointments in some areas but the success of the co-operative movement in the Scandinavian countries, especially Denmark, is very encouraging. The Danish co-operative movement has made a name for itself because of its close links with education without which it would not have been nearly so successful. This is a very important point which the fostering co-operative movements must not ignore.

Skilled manpower

Skilled labour is needed urgently throughout Africa as it is essential for the prosecution of the national development plans. This section of manpower fills the gap between the few specialized professionals and technologists and the mass of semi-skilled and unskilled labour. Skilled personnel are important for giving support to the professional workers and technologists, and also for focusing the ambitions of the semi-skilled working population.

Skilled manpower, however, has to be trained and there are no short cuts in the training process which in some fields takes years. A wise government will give as much attention to this aspect of national development as to the matter of national unity. A well-planned national development plan should include among its priorities the training of men and women in all fields. The development of technical schools and polytechnics should be regarded as an important priority and specific targets should be set in the production of technical manpower. The fields in which training is given priority will, of course, depend on the needs of the nation concerned.

It is difficult to draw the line between semi-skilled and skilled work but for a man to be considered skilled he must be trained in some functional activity. The place where this training takes place does not seem to matter. It could be on the job, or in the class-room. What is important is that the person concerned is gaining skills not by trial and error but through planned and systematic instruction of both theory and practice.

In the developing countries the importance of this section of the community is that it forms the bulk of those who have come into contact with technology and are therefore 'liberated'. They are in the front line of development. It is for this reason that this section of society forms the most formidable pressure group and it is the skilled worker who is the most important constituent of trade unions. For this reason his training should be planned not only in relation to civil and political responsibility but should also include instruction in the political objectives of the nation and the means to achieve these objectives. The workers' educational programme is an essential part of community development in the new states of Africa. It must be emphasized, however, that this form of education has its own objectives and its own different problems. Education of this type should be broad enough to include understanding of civic responsibility. It should help the worker to be in touch with his world and enable him to see his work in relation to the broad objectives of his nation.

The fact that the skilled-worker group is the main constituent of trade unions places responsibility upon those who lead trade unions to encourage and inspire the workers to increase their knowledge of their particular skills and to broaden their perspectives. While it is not necessarily the responsibility of trade union organizations to establish institutions for the training of workers, it is to their advantage to have well-informed and disciplined workers. This brings stability and increased productivity, which in turn creates a suitable climate for industrial prosperity, which is essential for national development.

Voluntary agencies and individuals should be encouraged to provide educational facilities for workers, but employers and governments must show interest and support. The formation of workers' educational associations whose main purpose would be to provide opportunities for workers to improve themselves by keeping them in touch with new ideas and developments related to their particular profession and with the development in the world in general should be encouraged. These associations could run programmes of informal education in seminars, conferences and forums in which all workers might be encouraged to take part. Financial support of these organizations could be mobilized from various national sources, including the employers. Since voluntarism is an essential part of the concept of a workers' educational organization, there should be minimum reliance on national funds, which are in any case already stretched to the utmost. Charitable organizations should always be encouraged to undertake workers' educational programmes.

Educated manpower

The term 'educated manpower' should be used with reserve because it is liable to lead to misunderstanding. It is used only as a differentiation from skilled manpower and is not meant to imply the existence of a group of workers who are 'uneducated manpower'. The term 'educated manpower' attempts to identify that vital group in modern society which supplies essential learned and scientific services in contrast to practical and technical services. These are men and women who have been specifically trained in the various professions: doctors, lawyers, architects, dentists, geologists, agricultural scientists, secondary school and university teachers, engineers and scientists. To this list should also be added the top administrators. For these posts some sort of professional training is required after a university or equivalent form of academic education. The main sources of this manpower are the universities, institutes of technology and specialist professional institutions. It is therefore necessary that these institutions of higher learning should be controlled by the state so that they can be brought into harmony with the national development plan and so that they will produce the type of man who will increase the effectiveness of the plan and will contribute to the achievement of national goals. State control of private institutions could take many forms. Where these institutions draw state subsidies for their operation it will seem logical for the state to require certain standards to be maintained and to know what is taught and even how it is taught. The importance of this force of 'educated manpower' lies not in the numbers involved but in the influence this group wields. In the new African states it is this section of the community which seems to determine the direction and tone of development, and from this group come the political leaders and top level administrators of the new nations.

Manpower planning is of even more importance when it comes to the consideration of 'educated manpower'. In this area, both under-estimation and over-estimation of requirements can have disastrous results. For example, a shortage of high-level manpower delays economic growth unless a large scale recruitment of expatriate staff is undertaken. On the other hand, uncontrolled manpower production tends to result in a surplus in certain professional areas, leaving more crucial areas understaffed. This can lead to a devaluation of professional skills resulting in frustration and social discontent.

The problem is estimating the 'educated manpower' needs of the national economic plans. The question is complicated by the fact that there are many factors, some of which may not be known at the time of planning, which will influence the situation. There have been a number of suggestions as to how a developing country can ascertain its high-level manpower requirement. The best known method is that put forward by Arthur Lewis, a West Indian educationalist. His formula is not only scientific, but is also relevant to the conditions of developing nations in Africa. In the paper which he presented to the Conference of African States on Education in 1961 entitled 'Education and Economic Development',[1] Lewis used a mathematical formula to determine the proportion of the population who should be receiving secondary and university education. On this basis he suggested, for example, that Nigeria should provide secondary education for 2·4% of her population and that the proportion which should go on to university education is 0·2%. These figures would apply to other countries in Africa which are at a similar stage of development.

A manpower forecast for any country must take many factors into account. It must consider the resources of the country, both potential and actual, and national goals and expectations. It must also take into account wastage and replacement, since in many countries the replacement of expatriate manpower is a real and serious problem.

In an ideal situation there should be a balance between the supply and demand of manpower, but this is rarely the case. For a start, the human element in calculations can never be accurately predicted. The training of manpower is one thing, the retaining of educated manpower is quite another. The developing countries are already experiencing the phenomenon of the 'brain-drain' or exodus of scientists and technologists to foreign countries where opportunities are greater. It is sometimes argued that the movement of scientists and professional persons has beneficial effects on international understanding and in the dissemination of knowledge, but while this is true to some extent for developed countries, a professional exodus can have disastrous repercussions on a new nation. It is expensive to produce men with reasonable professional qualifications in Africa and this training takes a sizeable proportion of the national income. For this reason everything possible should be done to keep trained manpower within the country. This is also important from the point of view of establishing national professional traditions. Therefore to retain high level professionals, a country must create a favourable climate for them. The reasons why highly-trained men emigrate are not only financial; some of those who decide to move to another country are attracted by conditions which enhance their profession or are merely seeking adventures.

One of the most serious problems new nations face in Africa is therefore that of competing on the world market for high calibre personnel. African salary structures have, of necessity, to be kept within the framework of the national economy. On the other hand, it is essential to keep on as many local professionals as possible during the process of taking over from expatriate personnel so as to maintain continuity and standards. In some countries a system of bonding has been tried as a means of keeping local professionals, but this is often not satisfactory as it places a man in a situation where he does not give of his best but merely buys time. The only hope is to make the work more challenging, to hold out more prospects of advancement and to give reasonable monetary rewards.

NOTES

1. Final Report of the Conference of African States on the Development of Education in Africa.

8

Conclusion

This inquiry has brought us to a number of conclusions. First, that the problems which led to the crisis in education in Africa are rooted in its historical development. Secondly, that leaders in education are right in their evaluation of the place and significance of education in all aspects of national development. Thirdly, that curriculum reform is a major priority in African education in order to make it relevant to the needs of a technological age. Fourthly, that the needs of the new nations are so many and so urgent that African states have to look to outside sources for aid in this gigantic task. Fifthly, African education is now an international concern; the pressure of these needs and the urgency of meeting them has made co-operation among the African states themselves necessary. Sixthly, that the cumulative effect of this crisis in education has created a serious shortage of manpower and placed limitations upon the speed and scope of development. The plans for educational development have so far not fulfilled forecasts and much still remains to be done. It must be said, however, that a number of African states have come near to realizing their goals in this field. The value of these plans lies in the fact that they give the African states objectives and so prepare them to face a gigantic task with resolve. To this end the plans have achieved something of what they were intended to do. Finally, the thinking of the new nations on adult education has been explored. Much is now being done to meet the needs of the adult community and most African states are giving adult education programmes the support they need.

Historical perspective of the crisis in education

The root cause of the crisis in African education lies in its historical development. In this respect the early history of education in Africa is inseparably bound up with the history of the Christian missions. We have therefore tried to consider educational problems in their historical perspective. The Cambridge Conference on African Education, 1952, seems to prove the validity of this point. While the Phelps-Stokes Commission called attention to the reality of the crisis, it was the Cambridge Conference which undertook to analyse the factors contributing to it. The Cambridge Conference helps us to see the whole problem of education in relation not only to its future development but also to the efforts of Christian missions in the development of education in Africa. Up to this point in history, it was being assumed by missions that education was an important aspect of evangelism, while the colonial governments considered it as an invaluable means of providing effective administration by the production of junior administrators and others in professions necessary for the promotion of order and good government. It was assumed that in this way civilizing influences would be maintained in the respective colonial territories.

The bounds of both these objectives were forcibly broken by the phenomenal demand for popular education which rendered the system intended to underguard and foster those aims completely inadequate. The Cambridge Conference shows clearly the seeds of this frustration and illustrates the divergent opinions about the means by which educational problems were to be solved. We see, for instance, a strong conviction that the problems were not to be solved by the building of more and more schools – this view had strong support especially among Africans themselves – but by an efficient organization, by the improvement of existing schools and by increasing a better-trained and well-equipped teaching force.

We have also observed that in recent years there has been a serious questioning of the aims of African education. The old 'omnibus' definition which defined education as 'an all-round development of the individual' has collapsed. The present question is how this all-round development can be related to the everyday life of the individual in the face of societies undergoing rapid social and political change.

It must be admitted that no satisfactory aim for education in Africa has as yet been worked out. Africa is in need of objectives in education big enough to transcend material achievements, for the needs of man in Africa, as everywhere else, are much more than material. We have noted with appreciation that the Addis Ababa Conference was not oblivious to the wider value of education and recognized that true education was that which helped to bring development of all aspects of human life, of which economic development was only a part. Notwithstanding this, however, the Addis Ababa Plan is intentionally biased towards the acquisition of technical skills, as these contribute directly to economic development. In all the discussions of the conference and in the plans themselves there is little evidence of concern for the fundamental factors which underlie the present pressure for a new evaluation of educational systems in Africa. It must therefore be concluded that this is a task which awaits attention and serious thinking, and this may be the vital role which African educators themselves will play in the coming years.

The Role of education in nation-building

The development of education has been through many changes, sometimes because of unprecedented social and political changes. This has been a necessary process because of the need to help the people of Africa to adjust to new conditions. The process of educational adaptation, however, has lagged behind the process of the African revolution. The result has been a feeling of helplessness and impatience on the part of the new nations for whom independence has held out hopes far beyond what can actually be achieved with existing resources in the time that has been available. Frustration has also arisen because evolution to nationhood has proceeded at a speed altogether out of proportion to the necessary leadership development. Many African countries are attempting development plans while greatly handicapped by a lack of manpower at all levels. It is therefore understandable that African states should take the view of education that they have. Educational programmes are aimed to meet the national requirements for trained men and women. In overcoming this problem planning is of the greatest importance.

Needs must be assessed, possibilities and potentialities examined and priorities established.

We are in agreement with the decisions on priorities which were made by the Addis Ababa Conference, especially those on the expansion of secondary education. This can be justified, first, on the basis that such expansion is the key to the manpower production problem, and secondly, because the development of higher education depends on the existence of a good secondary education system. However, a wider view of secondary education is important. It must be strengthened by sound educational principles which take serious account of the individuals involved. Education is a basis for economic development but should not, because of this, lose its freedom and become only nation-centred.

Curriculum reform

Most curricula in Africa at present have been transplanted from those Western countries with which the territories were linked through colonial administration. While these systems have contributed in a great measure to the raising of educational standards, they have at the same time tended to be inflexible and unable to penetrate the traditions and societies amongst which the African has to live. They have also tended to be superficial. This situation is aggravated by an undue emphasis on examinations, which has robbed the teacher of freedom to enrich a child's knowledge with experience of his community heritage.

The first step in the task of curriculum reform is therefore one of the re-orientation of African education so as to establish firmly its social and cultural basis. Fears have sometimes been expressed that this desire to bring education into harmony with African life may prove to be a retrogressive step. This view persists in spite of the fact that many students of African culture and society have again and again demonstrated convincingly the dynamic character of these societies and the ability of the peoples of Africa to adjust to new conditions and to undergo and accept change. Education brings into these cultures the element of progressive change. Reform is particularly needed in teaching attitudes and methods. New text books and materials must be prepared which will take into account the social and cultural environment of the African child.

International perspective

From the study of the Outline Plans for African Educational Development, both short and long term, it has been concluded that the needs are so urgent and so vast that African states on their own cannot adequately meet them. The foresight shown by the African nations in appealing to sources outside Africa for help is to be commended, as are the pledges for inter-African co-operation in efforts to safeguard educational systems and so promote plans for expansion. Thus the magnitude of the educational problem and the urgent need to meet the challenge it presents have brought in the third phase in the history of African educational development, namely the internationalization of African education. So far, however, there has been little inter-African co-operation in the matter of education as each nation seems to be too overwhelmed with its own internal problems.

There must be imaginative educational planning on a vast scale so that a much higher proportion of the population can be catered for. This planning, if it is to be effective, must take into account such factors as the shortage of teachers, classrooms and materials, as well as the economic structure into which the products of the increased educational facilities are to be integrated. The bias of African educational planning towards technical education is something that should be welcomed as this is bound to change the values in society, but these material values must be seen in relation to the needs of the whole man. Again, there are enormous problems which hamper efforts for planned development, especially in the drive for expansion of higher education facilities such as the establishment of new universities. Among these problems are lack of money and the inadequate output of the existing secondary schools which means that there are insufficient recruits for university institutions.

In these plans for the expansion of all forms of education, there is one gap which can only be ignored at the risk of creating instability in the new societies. This gap is the inadequate provision for a vigorous programme of agricultural education. African nations are essentially rural, as can be shown by the fact that most countries have on average more than ninety-five per cent of the population living in rural communities. Consequently, any economic plan which overlooks this fact is doomed to failure. Greater efforts should therefore be made in the development of agricultural education.

The responsibility for adult education for many years has been the province of voluntary agencies. The capacity and resources of these agencies are completely inadequate to operate a vigorous and effective programme of adult education and it must therefore of necessity be the responsibility of the state. We anticipate that the states concerned will naturally exercise control over all forms of adult education and will give it the support it requires.

The cumulative effect of this crisis in education has created a serious problem of shortage of manpower at all levels and unless there is careful planning of the use of available manpower resources all development plans will be handicapped. The answer to this diffi-culty seems to lie in the deliberate and serious planning of the development of personnel and the direction of manpower resources in a manner that will put to the most effective use the few men and women with skills and training that are available. Vigorous plans of selection and training must be mounted. Governments should exercise a measure of control in the training of personnel to avoid overlapping facilities and also to ensure that training is for the benefit of the country. Universities must be encouraged to diversify their professional faculties and there should exist in some form some kind of training in administration, as educated manpower is crucial to the development projects. Agricultural education at a university level should also be part of university expansion, and agricultural professional schools should be considered seriously by educators and governments.

In closing this inquiry, we would wish to express optimism over the development of education in Africa. The problems are enormous but they are not insurmountable and the future seems to be bright. African nations stand at the threshold of a new era in their history of educational development, and, given the necessary resources, they have the will to press on to achieve their aims. Education is indeed the key to the stored-up potential of human resources which all the African states have. This optimism, however, must be tempered by a critical evaluation of the systems and plans of education in rela-tion to the needs of the people and the realities of African condi-tions, and education must be seen in this respect as a basis for the development of the modern man in Africa. This task is a very great one and will require the mobilization of all available resources. It is too big a task for governments alone, even with the help of voluntary agencies. International concern for the development of Africa must now express itself in practical co-operation and assistance in the field of education.

INDEX

Addis Ababa
  Conference of African States on
    the Development of Education
    in Africa (1961), xvf., 27, 28, 32ff.,
    40, 41ff., 44, 45, 46f., 49, 51,
    53f., 57, 58, 61, 63, 64, 68, 72,
    77, 99, 104, 105
  Second Conference of Independ-
    ent African States (1960), 31
Adult education, 51, 55, 56, ch.6
    passim
  curriculum in, 82ff.
  teachers in, 86ff.
Advisory Committee on Education
  in the Colonies (1924), 15, 18, 22
Africa Literature Centre, 62
'African Personality', 35
African studies, importance of, 73
Agricultural education, 67f., 106f.
All African Conference of
    Churches, 56
  Bureau of Christian Education, 56
American Bible Society, 8
Angola, 3, 70

Baptist Missionary Society, 7
Belgium, 16
Berlin Convention (1885), 29f.
British & Foreign Bible Society, 7f.
British Somaliland, 23
British West Africa, 9, 13
Burundi, 70

Cambridge Conference on African
    Education (1952), 23ff., 32, 33,
    34, 61, 64, 103
  East and Central Africa Study
    Group, 24f., 61
  West African Study Group, 24

Cameroons, 66, 70, 82
Carey, William, 7
Catechists, 5f., 11
Catholic missions, 5f., 17
Christian Education in Africa,
    Conference on (1963), 53ff.
Church Missionary Society, 7, 9
Church of Scotland Missionary
    Committee, 8
Colonial administration, 10, 11, 91f.
'Comity' agreements, 9
Conference of Ministers of State
    on the Development of Educa-
    tion, 14
Congo, 3f., 5, 13, 16, 30, 66, 67, 70,
    71
Co-operative movement, 96
Correspondence schools, 80
Crowther, Samuel Adjai, 9
Cultural development, 34ff., 51
Curriculum reform, 51, 61ff., 105

Dahomey, 71
Dar-es-Salaam
  Kivukoni College, 82
  University College, 72
Diago Cao, 3f.

Edinburgh and Glasgow Missionary
    Society, 7
Educational planning, 44ff.
  co-operation between church and
    government, 15, 16
  and economic development, 39ff.,
    44ff.
Ethiopia, 17, 30, 67, 71
Evangelism, 3, 7, 8, 12, 39
Extra-mural studies, 73, 80f., 85f.